Speak
Lord
I'm Learning to Listen

Lyfe Publishing

Publishers Since 2012

Published by Lyfe Publishing LTD

Lyfe Publishing, 10800 Nautica Place, White Plains MD 20695

Library of Congress Cataloging in Publications Data

Sterns Wilson, Shawn-Ta

    Speaking Lord/Shawn-Ta Sterns Wilson

ISBN 978-0-578-52443-6

1. Inspirational/Motional – Non-Fiction
2. Christian – Non-Fiction
3. Religious – Non-Fiction

Printed in the United States of America

1 2 3 4 5 6 7 8 9 10

Book design by Olivia Pro Designs and Aionios Designs

Dedication

This book is dedicated to my girls:

Jordan – my daughter

Swanniqua – my goddaughter

If only you knew how often I thank God for blessing me with you.

I love you and I am proud of you!

CONTENTS

INTRODUCTION

DAY 1 NO SPOTS, NO BLEMISHES   8

DAY 2 COVERED AND PROTECTED   13

DAY 3 ACQUIESCE   20

DAY 4 INCOMPLETE INTERPRETATION   27

DAY 5 GIFT CARD   31

DAY 6 HIS WAYS   36

DAY 7 NOT MY CAR   47

DAY 8 CAMP   54

DAY 9 SUBTITLE   58

DAY 10 ANSWER THE CALL   63

DAY 11 FACEBOOK   68

DAY 12 DISTRAUGHT   74

DAY 13 SIMPLE OBEDIENCE   80

DAY 14 RAGS TO RICHES   90

DAY 15 ESP IS A GOD THING   96

DAY 16 A WALK WITH GOD   100

DAY 17 THY RIGHT HAND   105

DAY 18 BREATHING EASY   109

DAY 19 BROKEN   114

DAY 20 NOT TODAY DEVIL   118

DAY 21 THE MESSAGE WAS STILL VALID   124

DAY 22 THE WORD   129

DAY 23 AUGUST DEFINING MOMENTS   136

DAY 24 LADIES ENCOURAGING LADIES   148

DAY 25 STOP TALKING   155

DAY 26 SURVIVAL BY FAITH   166

DAY 27 WORK   173
DAY 28 MISSED OPPORTUNITY   178
DAY 29 WHEN ROOMING GOES WRONG   184
DAY 30 OUR THOUGHT LIFE MATTERS   190
DAY 31 WHEN HE LEADS I FOLLOW   196
BONUS STORY: WHO AM I?   210
FINAL THOUGHT   218
ABOUT THE AUTHOR   220

x

Acknowledgements

I can't image this book would be possible without the support and encouragement of my family, friends, and *Survival by Faith* supporters. To receive inquiries as to when 'the next book' would be published provided more encouragement than each of you could possibly imagine. Thank you for cheering me on to the finish line!

Introduction

Speak Lord

I'm Learning

to Listen

He that has an ear to hear, let him hear (Mark 4:9)

Just because someone has not accepted Christ does not mean Christ has not accepted them. After all, He made us all. I believe God speaks to all of His children, regardless of the depth of the relationship we have with Him. His desire is to see us be well - spiritually, physically, financially, emotionally, psychologically; in all ways. 3 John 2

1

"Beloved, I wish above all things that you prosper and be in health, even as your soul prospers. "I'm sure each of us desires that – to prosper in all ways – but we don't always know how to achieve it. God attempts to guide us. The word 'attempts' was used intentionally. While God certainly does speak, we often don't listen and therefore miss the guidance He is trying to give.

There are a myriad of reasons we may not hear God when He speaks. However, I believe we can safely sum them all up with these top three reasons:

❖ Can't: We aren't listening because we can't. The distractions of the world around us have hindered our ability to clearly hear and distinguish His voice.

❖ Won't: We aren't listening because we don't want to. It has happened to me many times where the word God spoke was not the word I wanted to hear. In some of those cases, I made the wrong decision and willfully did not obey. When we choose to that, please know in advance that there will be regret for making such a conscientious choice like that. Obeying may be where many people get tripped up. What God has to say is not always what we want to hear so we find ways to rationalize around it.

❖ Don't know how: We aren't listening because we simply don't know how. We have to learn to decipher His voice from our own. More importantly, is to decipher His voice from that of the enemy. That is guidance we certainly do not want to follow…ever!

Regardless of which category fits you most often, I assure you there is hope. It simply takes a conscientious effort to work on listening. This book has been written with one specific purpose in mind: to assist on your journey to discernment.

When we are in tune with the voice of the Lord we can take advantage of the direction and wisdom He is sharing with us. If we can't hear His voice over all the distractions in the world, we can miss out on wonderful moments He has in store for us. It can also leave us vulnerable to making wrong choices. There is no mistake-free or trouble-free living so let me not give that impression. However, in our mistakes and in our troubles, He will guide and lead us IF we listen…and then obey!

Before I understood all of this I would often say, "Something in my gut" told me to do or not to do a particular thing. Has that ever happened to you? That's God by way of the Holy Spirit. 1 John 2:20 speaks of the unction from the Holy One.

It is important to know God speaks, leads, guides, and teaches by way of the Holy Spirit. The role of the Holy Spirit is a deep study that I would encourage you to do at some point if you haven't already. To live our best and fullest life possible, learning to listen is crucial.

At times, the voice of God is so crystal clear there is no mistaking it for anything else. Where we can become confused or disheartened is in the times we presume His silence means He is not speaking. That may not be the case at all. Discernment is critical to our spiritual development.

As you read the stories contained herein, you will see that God speaks in a variety of ways; some you may be well acquainted with through your own personal experiences.

In my quest for oneness with God, I have found writing to be extremely beneficial. When we are in the moment of life, it can be hard to clearly see things for what they are as they occur. Hindsight gives us a much better perspective on the broad scope of intertwined situations we may have thought to be isolated incidents.

I whole-heartedly encourage you to read the stories and go through the writing exercise as well. Your daily notes may prove to be invaluable later in seeing your blessings (encounters, answers, guidance, revelation, etc.) unfold over a period of time.

If you're searching for answers, please remember that God's timing reigns supreme. Answers may not come as quickly as we like. This is another reason capturing thoughts and experiences daily will be helpful. Answers sometimes come in the form of building blocks: "this" has to happen before "that" can happen, and so on until the full answer is revealed or understanding is gained. Or, as is written in Isaiah 28:10 "For precept must be upon precept, precept upon precept; line upon line, line upon line; here a little, and there a little."

Learning to listen also entails watching the actions of others. Learn to listen to what their actions show you in addition to their words. Actions speak louder than words; it's likely you have heard that expression many times. Learn to listen to actions. Answers can be found there also.

Throughout the pages of my first book, *Survival by Faith*, I documented the details of the most challenging year of my life. Challenging as it may have been, I learned a lot about God and how He feels about me by His actions towards me that year. While He spoke not a word for twelve consecutive months, His actions told me many things. A few of which were:

1. He was with me. Although He was silent, He was there because He comforted me.

2. He loved me. I could tell this by the way He kept keeping me. When I thought I could take no more, He held me up and that was the only way I could stand.

3. He provided for me. When finances were an issue, He made a way for me to take care of my responsibilities.

One last reminder before you embark on your journey to discernment: please remember to write your daily notes. They will reveal more than you may anticipate!

Day 1
No Spots, No Blemishes

A few years ago I had two blemishes on my face that seemed to appear overnight. One was on my nose and the other was directly above my upper lip. I put fading cream on them from time to time but not on a consistent basis so they remained. I would like to think that my lackluster efforts to make them disappear were because I'm simply not a vain person. Some days they bothered me more than others when I saw them. Generally speaking, however, I didn't really notice them until I decided to focus on them. I had gotten used to them being there.

8

While at a red light one morning, I looked in the mirror. At that particular moment, the blemishes seemed to be larger than life! Without hesitation, I touched each one and prayed that the Lord would remove each spot/blemish. As soon as I did, He quickened me in the spirit and asked this: "Are you as concerned about your spiritual spots and blemishes or just the natural ones?" I immediately repented.

We all have spiritual blemishes and I would dare say we are even aware of them. Yet, how much do we focus on removing them? I can only speak for myself when I say there is room to do more. Don't get me wrong, I am concerned on a daily basis about my spirituality because it is tied directly to my eternity and I can't play around with that! But, just as I noticed the spots on my physical body which caused me to pause and pray for their removal, I should be able to recognize the spots and blemishes in my spirit. Once recognized, it is even more important to be concerned with removing them.

We can get so accustomed to living with our spiritual blemishes that they don't bother us and that's dangerous. Going about our day-to-day lives without working to remove these blemishes keeps us from living our best life possible, and could keep us from our place in the Kingdom. We've held a grudge for such a long time that it has settled comfortably in our spirit. We were hurt and the spot the pain left on our heart has not healed because we can't let go until the person apologizes. We all know how seldom that happens. Worst of all, because of what they did, we shield ourselves from getting close to anyone else, which leaves us lonely and feeling isolated. Or, we've dated a person for so long, engaged in all levels of intimacy outside of marriage that we've even fooled ourselves into believing it is okay because it is at least a monogamous relationship.

These are all spiritual blemishes in God's eyes. The blessing is that He has given us the best fading cream of all - His word! If we can become more consistent in applying it generously to our daily lives, I guarantee the spots and blemishes will begin to fade away! He'll show us how to forgive. He'll show us how to trust again. He'll show us how to love and be loved the right way. We won't be

10

perfect because only God can be and is that. We'll still make mistakes and stumble because we are human. But, we will be operating with a pure heart.

What happened to the blemishes on my face? By the grace of God, one is completely gone and the other hardly visible! Of course, I am choosing to believe that as I work on my spiritual blemishes, God is blessing me by working on my natural ones!

Day 1 - Moment of Reflection:

Are there any spiritual blemishes you can work on?

_____

_____

_____

_____

_____

_____

_____

_____

_____

_____

_____

_____

_____

_____

_____

_____

_____

Day 2

Covered &

Protected

The day I did my first radio interview to discuss one of my books, I was a bit nervous. The entire book publishing experience had taken me far outside of my comfort zone. I function best behind the scenes, helping to make things happen for others. Being interviewed was new for me and put me more front and center than I was accustomed to. Comfortable or not, when the opportunity presented itself to speak about the book on radio, I jumped on it. I was nervous but said yes. The book was an assignment given to me by God. Promoting His project was more important than my comfort.

For marketing and promotional purposes, I thought it would be a good idea to have someone take a few pictures during the interview. Unfortunately, and quite uncharacteristically, I waited until the last minute to ask anyone to come along. All three last-minute attempts failed. That didn't concern me too much. Between the radio host and myself, I knew we could capture a couple of good shots. In the back of my mind, however, I was hoping someone could join me for the sheer company and to provide a little support and encouragement. Radio was new for me and I wasn't sure how I would do.

On the way there, one of the three people I contacted earlier in the day called. Her plans had changed and she was now available to go with me. By the time I received her call, I had already left home and was halfway to the station. There was still plenty of time for her to meet me there and I was tempted to suggest that. Something in my spirit was telling me to leave well enough alone though.

I thanked her but let her know it was okay and I'd be fine on my own.

As I got closer to the station there were a few powerful gospel songs that played back-to-back on the satellite radio channel I listen to. The music was shifting my focus from the interview to worship!

When I reached my destination, my plan was to sit in the car for a few minutes and make phone calls. There was time to spare since I arrived early. The music in the car continued to minister to me. Even so, I found myself reaching for the button to turn it off in order to make my phone calls. Immediately I sensed I was not supposed to. Instead of turning the music off I said, "Ok Lord. I don't know what this is about but ok." He was doing something within me by way of song and silence. I was able to recognize that much even though I had no clue what He was doing or why. Even without knowing the reason, I knew enough to listen and obey. Whenever I have occurrences like this happen I can typically look back later and realize it was for my own good. Seeing it, hearing it, feeling it, recognizing it as it is happening is often the hard part. Once I've identified that 'God is up to something' as people like to say, I know it is in my best interest to go along with His plan!

Once it was time, I walked into the station and felt at ease. Whatever nerves I had were gone. There was no longer any apprehension about the new experience I was about to have. Actually, a little excitement started to kick in.

Mid-way through the interview, the radio host shared some information with me off the air. She let me know a group of atheists would be using the studio immediately after our segment. She continued on by saying she was feeling a heaviness in her spirit because of their presence. The group arrived early for their show and was now waiting in the lobby for us to finish. At one point, the host had to stop and pray silently while I continued answering her last question on air. Whatever she was sensing in her spirit was real and she needed to deal with it. Although I was not impacted by their presence in the same way, I absolutely respected what she needed to do to guard herself spiritually.

When my interview was over, the host and I walked out of the sound booth. I was able to smile sincerely and speak to the handful of folks who were sitting in the lobby waiting for their airtime. By the grace of God, my spirit was not bothered by their presence at all.

Driving home, I realized what all the one-on-one time in the car with God was all about. He was strengthening me and fortifying my spirit against those which would be present at the station. I am grateful God covered and protected me before I even walked in the door!

Had I asked my friend to come along since her plans changed last minute, it is likely we would have spent the drive and early arrival time talking and laughing. The gospel station is always on in my car no matter who is with me, but it is unlikely I would have been focused on what was playing and how God was trying to get my attention before entering the radio station for the interview.

Upon my arrival, had I proceeded with turning the radio off to make phone calls when I knew He was telling me not to, it is also quite likely I would not have received the covering and strengthening He blessed me with before entering the building. God knew the environment I would be walking into; I didn't. He did what He needed to do in order to cover and protect me. God made sure I was not left exposed and vulnerable to spiritual agitation.

I love all the wonderful ways He works in our lives if we just let Him.

I dare not consider the impact the spirit of doubt and rebellion the atheists carry could have had on me. Don't turn the radio off. Take this ride by yourself. The guidance seems too minuscule to have come from God, right? The Holy Spirit leads and guides in a multitude of ways. Obedience to the little things can be as critical to our spiritual well-being as obedience to the big things. Listen! No matter the instruction. When God speaks, He has a purpose behind it and it is always designed for our good and/or the good of others through us.

Day 2 - Moment of Reflection:

Have you ever sensed a time God wanted to spend one-on-one time with you? Did you set the time aside?

_____

_____

_____

_____

_____

_____

_____

_____

_____

_____

_____

_____

_____

_____

_____

_____

Day 3

Acquiesce

As I was in the shower one day, God asked me, "How much of the world are you going to acquiesce to? I've called you to be different." My spirit was immediately convicted because I knew what He was referring to. I had sold myself short in order to be in a relationship with a man. I let my standards down and accepted things I knew were not pleasing to God.

When God speaks to me in these ways, I am immediately reminded of His word. I am blessed to have been taught so much of His word over the years. A true Bible-teaching

20

church is vital to our walk with God. That obviously does not mean we will not stumble because we will. What it does mean, however, is we know where to draw our strength from during times we feel ourselves falling short. The word of God helps us get back up, dust ourselves off, ask for forgiveness (with a sincere heart), and move on. When we know better we do better! His gentle and loving reminders, like the one He gave me in the shower, encourage us to do better.

I had become way too comfortable living according to the world's standards and not God's. I had conformed even when I knew I shouldn't. Two scriptures, in particular, came to me that morning:

I Peter 2:9 (KJV) But ye are a chosen generation, a royal priesthood, an holy nation, a peculiar people; that ye should shew forth the praises of him who hath called you out of darkness into his marvelous light.

Romans 12:2 (KJV) And be not conformed to the things of this world: but be ye transformed by the renewing of your mind, that ye may prove what is that good, and acceptable, and perfect, will of God.

But I loved him. Did you notice the lower case 'h' in him? I loved the man so I justified in my mind why it was okay to conduct our relationship in an inappropriate manner. Beating around the bush has never been one of my specialties so let me not try to start now. I justified in my mind why it was okay that we had sex and I stayed the night at his house and went on trips with him with no accountability. Like I said, I loved him. That was supposed to make it acceptable in my mind and make me feel better. The truth of the matter is it did not; not on either account. It did not make me feel better and it surely was never acceptable to God.

There is no condemnation in Christ (Romans 8:1). Yet, when we truly have a desire to please God and live according to what He deems acceptable, we will feel bad once we realize we've fallen short. It's important then to understand the difference between condemnation and conviction. Condemnation is not from God. It will leave you feeling guilty and less than. Conviction is an awareness of sin with a sincere desire to stop. When our heart is centered on pleasing God, the conviction will lead to correction. I felt a great sense of conviction the day the Lord spoke to me in the shower. I knew better but I had not done better. I was disappointed in myself as a result. It became so clear to me that my excuses were not fooling anyone, not even myself. How we receive His reminders determines what we do with them. It would have done no good to beat myself up over it. The only positive use of the reminder was to try and get back on track.

I was so torn. I wanted to please both of them; Him (God) and him (the man). But that's exactly where I made the mistake. We are not called to please man; we are called to please God (Galatians 1:10). Would he (the man) understand if the dynamics of our relationship changed? Would He (God) understand if they didn't? The answer to the first question was, at best, a 'maybe'. The answer to the second question seemed to be a resounding 'no' in my mind.

When we met and decided to see each other exclusively, I was frank about my wishes. I did not want to be intimate with another man unless he was my husband. Since my ex-husband, there had been no one else. Surely, this guy would respect that, right? Deep down I believed he would see it as admirable and have a different level of respect for me. The problem, as I saw it, was he was guided by flesh and the world's standards as well. He was leading and I was following but we were going in the wrong direction. "There is a way that appears to be right, but in the end it leads to death." Prov 14:12 (NIV)

That very well could be the reason the relationship died? Using our brilliant natural minds, we convinced ourselves we were okay, you know, because we were exclusive.

Living the world's way is much easier, I grant you that. Living life God's way is much more rewarding and peaceful, however! It requires meeting the daily challenge of conquering the flesh. We should always keep that at the forefront of your mind.

Renewing our minds is a daily necessity. The word of God is a tremendous help in that effort. Feeding our spirit with it as much as possible will lessen the desire to satisfy the flesh.

I don't enjoy telling the details of my personal life. I've said before, however, that there is no testimony without transparency. I share details of my experiences for enlightenment and encouragement, not for enjoyment or judgment. The struggle to stay right is real and matters of the heart are the hardest to overcome.

Day 3 - Moment of Reflection:

Which area of your life do you struggle most in maintaining God's standards?

_____

_____

_____

_____

_____

_____

_____

_____

_____

_____

_____

_____

_____

_____

_____

_____

_____

Day 4

Incomplete

Interpretation

"Watch out."

Huh?

"Watch out."

Although the words were spoken softly, I felt it was a message which required immediate application. There was no sense of urgency in the tone of the words spoken, yet they put me on instant alert!

I didn't know exactly why the Lord was warning me but since I was driving at the time, I decided to be a little extra aware of my surroundings on the road.

It's not unusual to see people running red lights downtown. Morning, afternoon, and evening it is a frightening and regular occurrence. With the message fresh in my mind, I approached the next intersection and slowed down. Initially, I looked to my left. The light in front of me was green but I thought it wise to be extra sure the cars coming from the left were not planning to run their red light.

God's warning was on point. I was supposed to be extra cautious. A second after looking to my left and seeing no cars running the red light, a car crossed in front of me from the RIGHT!! This vehicle was in the far right lane and attempted to make a left-hand turn across three lanes of traffic!

But by the grace of God, I did not hit the car. Although I slammed on my brakes my SUV never fully stopped because it slid after I hit the brakes. It is nothing short of a miracle my vehicle did not collide with the other. God's hand of protection certainly covered me.

In life, we sometimes know to be on the look-out but we think the danger or distraction is going to come from a specific direction. This showed me clearly that God is saying to keep our eyes open in ALL directions! God did not say "watch out from the left"; He simply said, "Watch out". It was my misconstrued thinking and faulty rationalizing that did not allow me to consider danger from all sides.

It did not dawn on me that danger may come from the right. The traffic pattern was not set-up for that. I received the warning spoken to my spirit but I made an assumption in thinking I knew where the danger would come from.

Don't get blind-sided. Heed the warning and take a panoramic view of what's going on around you. God sees the big picture and many times we do not. Yet, if we're listening, He may provide a warning!

Day 4 - Moment of Reflection:

In hindsight, and metaphorically speaking, have you ever been blindsided because you did not heed a spiritual warning, or assumed it meant one thing when it meant another?

_____

_____

_____

_____

_____

_____

_____

_____

_____

_____

_____

_____

_____

_____

_____

_____

Day 5
Gift
Card

Life gives me plenty of opportunities to laugh at myself in hindsight! Recently I had another.

My cousin is so sweet. She loves to cook and she loves to feed people. This works out really well in our relationship because I love to eat and hate to cook!

She hosted a small gathering at her home on the 4th of July. Although the number of guests was small, the amount of food was enough to feed an army. The next day, the

Lord put it on my heart to stop by the grocery store and buy a gift card for her. While there, I also purchased a thank you card. In the card, I wrote a small note to personally let her know I appreciate her "always feeding the army of us."

I wanted to hand-deliver the card the day I purchased it but she wasn't available. Not wanting to delay her receiving the gift, I drove to her house and placed it in her mailbox. I've done things like this before. It's nice to get a surprise every once in a while. I thought it would make her smile to get something unexpected.

As I pulled up to the mailbox, I started questioning if I should put the card in there or not. "What if someone sees me do this and takes the card", I thought. As quickly as the thought came to mind, I dismissed it. The funny thing is another, similar thought came to mind. I dismissed it as well.

The card was placed in her mailbox and I drove away. I knew she would be surprised and appreciative and call right away to say thanks. The entire evening went by, however, and she didn't call. The next day came and went with no mention of the card. Finally, on the third day, I asked if she had checked her mail recently. She had but said there was nothing out of the ordinary in there. When I told her I left something for her, she went through her mail once again. Still, she did not see the pink envelope with her name written on it.

It was gone!

While I was extremely disappointed she did not receive the gift intended for her, I also had to chuckle at myself. Although I had done things like this in the past, I wasn't supposed to do it THAT DAY! The Spirit of the Lord tried to warn me by putting questions in my spirit. I chose to ignore them. This time it only cost me $25 but not listening may not always be so inexpensive.

If the Spirit of the Lord gives you a moment of pause, please do exactly that; pause and recognize what He may be trying to tell you.

I, too, am still learning to listen.   It is a daily and often, moment-to-moment, conscientious effort to:

1. Remember that God speaks even concerning little things.

2. Recognize His leading at the moment.

3. Listen (obey).

Something so simple, yet He concerned Himself with it to spare me from losing the money spent and my cousin missing out on a blessing. Such a great example of how God is constantly watching over us.

I was frustrated with myself that day. Unlike some the frame of other stories shared within the pages of this book, this one took place at a time I considered myself much more in-tune with the voice of God. Shame on me! It just goes to show there will always be work to do in our quest for oneness with Him; and the work is on our part, not His!

Day 5 - Moment of Reflection:

Have you ever dismissed a gut feeling because it didn't make sense to you?

_____

_____

_____

_____

_____

_____

_____

_____

_____

_____

_____

_____

_____

_____

_____

_____

_____

_____

Day 6

His

Ways

Learning to listen involves learning to decipher God's will in the silent moments. In the silent moments, when we can't seem to hear God, our faith becomes critically important. When we believe what we are seeking is a 'good thing' yet it doesn't seem to be happening it can leave us feeling a little abandoned and confused. The word says that God will never leave us nor forsake us (Hebrews 13:15). Something I desperately desired was being denied to me. It would have been perfect for my family life so I deemed it a fitting example of a 'good thing' that God surely would not withhold from me, yet He did.

Scripture says no good thing will He withhold from those who walk uprightly (Psalm 84:11). So if we know it's a good thing and we are asking for it with a pure heart, why is it not happening?

There can be many reasons why. It could be God has decided the timing is not right. It could also be, even though we think something is good for us, it may not be. Or, could it be God has something much better in mind for us which we simply cannot conceive?

I was given an opportunity once to decipher God's will during a time of silence. I'll be completely transparent and tell you up front that I absolutely blew it. I'm talking about epic failure!

For 18 years my career required that I work a consistently irregular schedule. This could mean working three out of four weekends in a month; working 13 days in a row before a day off; as well as working nights and holidays. When my daughter reached high school, I felt a strong need to have a more regular schedule in order to maximize those four years with her.

There were no positions within my department that would afford me the same salary and a regular schedule. I love where I work, so looking for a job outside of my organization wasn't an option for me. To my surprise, soon after high school started, there was an opening in our Sales Office. The work schedule for that position was exactly what I needed; no weekends, no nights, no holidays, with Monday through Friday standard office hours only. The downside of that position was it required I accept a pay cut. The highest salary available for that pay scale was $10,000 less than what I was currently making.

I was so desperate for the normal work schedule that I applied for the job and sincerely wanted it, despite the pay cut. Having worked on the services side of our company for many years and thought the experience gained there would enhance my ability to be an excellent Sales Manager. In addition, I had recently remarried so the household had two incomes instead of one now. Although no one wants to lose $10,000 of their salary, I was comfortable making the change because I was no longer single and solely responsible for all household expenses.

Phone interviews were done first and I did very well. The next round was a personal interview. That went well also and I was optimistic the position would be offered to me. When a decision was made, the Director of Sales came to my office to let me know he was offering it to someone else. Hearing those words shocked me, especially since he told me how well I interviewed and he knew I could do the job. In his words, he was looking for someone with "real sales experience".

This is where I blew it. I lost sight of faith and became angry. It would have been a 'good thing' for me and my family so why did God not allow it to happen? I believed I was in a place (lifestyle and relationship with God) where I was living and walking uprightly, so why had He withheld the job from me? To be clear, I wasn't angry at God. I don't know if there has ever been a time in my life that

I've been angry at God. I was angry with the Director of Sales. I was angry about the situation I was still stuck in. What God does confuses me sometimes but I praise His Holy name that I've never felt anger towards Him for something that did or did not happen. I think I'm afraid to be angry with Him. He created me so He knows what He's doing with me. I just don't understand it a lot of times.

The anger soon turned to resentment and I distanced myself from the Director of Sales. My behavior towards him was immature and unprofessional. I was having such a hard time working through my feelings and they got the best of me. Hindsight is a great teacher. In looking back, I don't think I tried hard enough to work through how I felt. There were constructive measures I could have taken and I regret not doing so. I felt as though my last hope for balance in my personal life was gone when the position was given to someone else.

BUT GOD...

If in my mind, taking a $10,000 pay cut in order to have a Monday through Friday regular work schedule was a good idea, wouldn't it make sense that God just might have a bigger and better idea? After all, His thoughts are not like ours, neither are His ways (Isaiah 55:8) There were no positions within my company structured to offer the same pay I was currently making and provide a regular schedule. I could not see how God could work things out for my good but He surely was about to.

A year later our new Facility Director approached me and asked if I'd be interested in taking a position he was about to create. Not only was this a new position but I was being chosen for it. In his words "when I look at the staff currently on hand, you're the only one I believe can do this". Now, he is a businessman and the proverbial show must go on so he continued by saying, "but if you don't want it, I'll find someone else".

As we talked about the position it certainly seemed interesting. Initially, the interest was because it was new. However, when we got into the specifics of the job, I realized it was

41

primarily a Monday through Friday opportunity with regular hours. I couldn't believe it! More shocking than the schedule was the pay. It wasn't a pay increase but nor was it a pay cut. I was being offered what I didn't think existed. Actually, I was being offered something which never existed but was exactly what I needed at that particular stage in my life.

My reply was, "No need to find someone else. Yes, I'll take the position."

Oh, how I thank God for His grace and mercy! When it was all said and done I was able to reflect back and see how He had His loving hand on me and the situation the entire time. I was so upset with and ashamed of myself for how I acted when told I did not get the Sales position. It is truly only by the grace of God that, a year later, He saw fit to follow through with His plan and still bless me with the position which met all of my needs and wants!

Because of the way I had acted I had to ask God to forgive me. My actions had not been a good representation of Him at all. In addition to that, I had to ask the Director of Sales to forgive me as well. With transparency as a goal, I must say that I asked God for forgiveness immediately after being denied the position. As for the Director of Sales, that was a huge chunk of humble pie I had a hard time eating. I had been so distant towards him for an entire year. I was embarrassed at my behavior. Even if God had not blessed me with the perfect position, I still owed the Director of Sales an apology. My inner spirit man wanted to and knew I needed to but I battled doing it in the flesh.

When I was finally able to conquer the flesh (embarrassment/pride) and apologize to him, he accepted it and I thanked him.

Not long after being turned down for the Sales position, my short-lived marriage ended. Had I been hired for the job I professed to be a 'good thing', I would have sustained a $10,000 pay cut and been left in financial strain. Although I didn't know what was coming in terms of my marriage, God knew. He also knew that I wouldn't be able to take a hit like that financially.

These experiences have helped strengthen my faith. We won't always be able to see how things will work out. Situations can often times appear hopeless, but the key is to hold on and stay in faith! God has us in the palm of His ever-loving and mighty hand! If He denied the position I wanted, I should have had more faith and trust in Him to provide something better.

Now I find it hard to focus on what didn't happen. I am more accepting of the "no's" because God has shown me that it's quite possible He has better in store.

Although I'm certain I never heard the Spirit of the Lord speak to me about the matter, it was still an opportunity to listen. God's denial may not always be final! For all He has done over the course of my life, I owed it to Him to let it all play out. I owed it to God to give Him the benefit of the doubt that if He was saying no, there had to be a reason...a really good reason.

Faith and feelings operate very contrary to one another. I let my feelings, instead of my faith, dictate my response and subsequent actions, which I later regretted.

God will perfect that which concerns you. He promises that in Psalm 138:8. What on Him!

Day 6 - Moment of Reflection:

When was the last time you perceived a delay as God's denial?

_____

_____

_____

_____

_____

_____

_____

_____

_____

_____

_____

_____

_____

_____

_____

_____

_____

_____

_____

Day 7
Not
My Car

When I turned 48 I decided I would spend
the next two years saving and planning to buy
the car of my dreams for my 50th birthday.
There was no specific car I had in mind at the
time. The only requirement was I wanted
something I considered an upgrade.

Shortly after my 49th birthday, I ran into a car
salesman I knew. My current vehicle was due
for service. While waiting in the lobby, we ran
into one another. I reminded him that I would
be in the market for another car in less than a
year. We talked about cars I liked. That gave

me a chance to share with him that, of all the cars I've driven over the years, the Mercedes was my favorite. Once he heard that, he told me that he had a car on the lot he wanted me to see. Although I had no intention of buying a car that day, I was curious and wanted to see what he thought I would be interested in.

He walked me over to a black Mercedes. Although I had no idea what car I would end up buying, I knew I wouldn't purchase another dark colored car. Therefore, the first one he showed me did not appeal to me at all. Once I told him that I thought our browsing would be over. He didn't miss a beat. He asked me to continue walking and just a couple spaces over from the black Mercedes was another one. As soon as I saw it I stopped in my tracks, my mouth fell open, and I may have actually stopped breathing for a second or two. It was the most beautiful shimmery gold Mercedes I had ever seen! Once I regained composure the first words out of my mouth were something like, "I want that car!"

It was a used model with very low mileage and was so well kept it looked show-room new. I was in awe. I kept trying to talk myself out of being interested because it wasn't my 50th birthday yet. I had set a timeline for specific reasons but found myself struggling to remember them at the moment.

When our paths crossed that morning, he was in the middle of assisting another customer but had taken a few minutes to show me these vehicles. I had a full day of errands to run that day so it was not a convenient time for either of us. We agreed to meet the next day. Before leaving I remember saying to him "don't sell my car, I'm coming back for it tomorrow!" With every fiber of my being I meant those words.

When I returned to the dealership the next day I recall looking at the clock. It was exactly 3 pm when I parked. Many years ago the Bishop of our church said God gave him the 60-second prayer. The Lord instructed Bishop to have the people pray every hour on the hour for 60-seconds. When the 60-second prayer was first introduced to the church, many of us were faithful about keeping it. I would have to admit that, over time, I fell off from doing it regularly.

However, when I happen to notice it is the top of the hour, I do stop and pray.

Since it was 3 pm and I was about to make a major decision, I took full advantage of the 60-second prayer opportunity. In the prayer, I recall asking God to be with me as I made this decision and to make it easy for me to know what I should do. I really wanted the car but I needed to be sure it was a wise move on my part. The prayer lasted a few minutes instead of just one. (I'm sure God didn't mind that at all) When I finished praying, I got out of the car and was excited to go find the salesman. When we connected, the first thing I said, even before saying hello, was "you didn't sell my car did you?" He laughed and said, "No, it's right over there."

As we walked towards the car we talked about pricing and other details. I was even more excited when he told me the deal he thought he could give. All of that excitement faded quickly once we reached the location the car was parked. I was confused. I was looking at the car but for some reason, it didn't look like the same one as the day before. There was such a difference I asked him if he was sure this was the same vehicle from the day before. He said that it was and I believed him but it didn't look the same at all. Instead of being the shimmery gold I fell in love with, it now looked silver. We walked around the car and I looked at it from every angle possible and could not understand how it could look so different from one day to the next. None the less, it did and I was not pleased.

We took the car for a test drive and it drove wonderfully. Yet, when we got back to the lot, I still could not get over the color contrast. The salesman offered me an amazing deal for the car but even that didn't help. I didn't want it anymore.

I apologized to him and I left. It wasn't until I started driving home that I realized what had just happened. In my prayer, I asked God to "make it easy for me" in regards to knowing whether or not I should purchase the car. Well, He did exactly what I asked Him to do. It was one of the easiest decisions of my life. I was able to walk away with absolutely no regrets and never look back.

Even though He did not speak words into my spirit about the car, He definitely spoke to me in a way I would not misunderstand. God was adamant this particular car was not for me. Despite the great price and pristine condition of it, I would have been a fool to buy the car after the way the Lord turned my heart from it!

I am learning to listen to all the different ways He speaks. It is my belief that one of the keys to listening to God is to realize that He speaks in a variety of ways. It won't always be with softly spoken words via the Holy Spirit to our spirit. It could be changing our heart's desire for something He knows isn't good or His best for us. Have you ever just felt deep down inside that you should or shouldn't do something but couldn't explain why you felt that way? Yes, that's God speaking to your spirit as well. When you just know what you know but don't know why!

Day 7 - Moment of Reflection:

Do you consult God before making major decisions?

_____

_____

_____

_____

_____

_____

_____

_____

_____

_____

_____

_____

_____

_____

_____

_____

_____

Day 8
Camp

One summer when my daughter was middle school age, I let her stay home from camp on a particular Monday. Her birthday was over the previous weekend and it had been a full weekend of activity. I knew she was tired because I was, too!

It was a stretch for me to let her stay home one day by herself, but two days was certainly out of the question. Therefore, I knew I would be taking her to camp the next day.

For some reason, on Monday afternoon, I sensed in my spirit I should call to be sure the camp would be open Tuesday. It didn't make sense to me why they wouldn't be open so I did not make the call.

Tuesday morning as I was driving her to camp, the same thing hit my spirit: "You should call". Again I ignored it because my mind could not conceive why they would not be open on a Tuesday.

By now you may have figured out that when we arrived the camp was closed!

How many times has God tried to help you? He told you something and you ignored it? He leads and guides us in little and big ways. We just have to be ready and willing to listen. Had I listened, it would have saved me time, aggravation, even money on the toll road. Because I did not listen I was also late for work that day. After finding the camp closed, I had to take my daughter all the way back home before going to work.

Not listening put me in an uncomfortable position. I did not want my daughter staying

home two days in a row by herself but I left
myself no choice. Had I listened to the Spirit
of the Lord on Monday and called the camp, I
would have had an opportunity to find an
alternative plan for Tuesday. I guarantee my
daughter was tired of answering the phone
every thirty minutes as I called to check on
her.

None the less, I had to say, "Thank you Lord
for trying." He absolutely, 100%, without a
shadow of a doubt tried to spare me all of the
morning inconvenience and uneasiness I went
through all day.

He's faithful in helping us. We must get to the
point of being faithful in letting Him!

Day 8 - Moment of Reflection:

Has God spared you inconvenience by suggesting you verify an assumption you've made?

_____

_____

_____

_____

_____

_____

_____

_____

_____

_____

_____

_____

_____

_____

_____

Day 9
Subtitle

From the very beginning, I heard the Spirit of the Lord tell me the title and subtitle of the first book I published. He said, "*Survival by Faith – A Story of Faith, Obedience, and Revelation*".

That being the case, why did I let someone talk me out of including the subtitle? This is an excellent question, for which I have a poor answer. When God says what something should be, who is man to say otherwise?

In initial discussions with the publisher, I indicated the title of the book may or may not include a subtitle. When the cover was designed, the graphic artist included a subtitle as more of a place holder than an actual subtitle. The subtitle he wrote was based on a few sentences I shared about the book in order to give him a feel for the content and help come up with cover design options.

Mid-way through the project, I made the decision there would be no subtitle. This information was relayed so the graphic artist could update the cover by removing the place holder subtitle. When the book was finished, we went through three proof copies. Each came back with the place holder subtitle still on them. I was so frustrated that, after repeated requests, the cover still was not correct. It took four requests before receiving a proof which had the title listed as *Survival by Faith*, with no subtitle.

I now realize the Lord was gracious enough to give me a few opportunities to pause and reflect on what He had told me from the start regarding the title and subtitle. But, I blew it. Only in hindsight can I see clearly and recognize the experience for what it was. I was supposed to seek God in those moments and ask Him to help me understand why I was having such a hard time getting the subtitle taken off the book. Had I sought Him sincerely, I guarantee He would have brought back to my remembrance the direction He had given me from the onset. I would have then recognized that although the place holder subtitle was incorrect, a subtitle was to be included!

God was speaking by way of what I considered to be a human error. Little did I know it was divine intervention. Because I was operating in my feelings (frustrated, eager to publish, impatient and ready to complete my Kingdom assignment), I was not able to discern His direction. It's such a beautiful thing to see how many different ways He can deliver messages to us. We just have to be ready to listen regardless of the method He chooses to speak. After three failed attempts to get my attention, I can imagine God saying, "Well, I tried. She'll understand later."

A year after the initial release date, the book was re-released with the subtitle on the cover as given to me from the beginning; *"Survival by Faith – A Story of Faith, Obedience, and Revelation".*

It is so much better to heed the advice of scripture. The Bible is the word of God and is the believer's instruction book for life. Psalms 118:8 reminds us that it is "Better to trust in the Lord than put confidence in man." It became clear to me the consultant I hired to help me navigate the publishing process did not have pure motives. I could not see it at the time. I looked at their experience in the book publishing business and gave their opinion more weight than the voice of God. I am embarrassed to admit to that. My lack of confidence hindered me from listening to what I heard so clearly in my spirit.

Life is a journey and God is there with us every step of the way. He endeavors, through the leading of the Holy Spirit, to help us, lead us, and guide us. Placing the voice of the Lord above all others is our responsibility in our relationship with Him.

Day 9 - Moment of Reflection:

Has God given you multiple opportunities to stop and hear Him through circumstances?

_____

_____

_____

_____

_____

_____

_____

_____

_____

_____

_____

_____

_____

_____

_____

_____

_____

_____

_____

Day 10
Answer
the Call

Ms. Bernie was such a special woman. Although we had only known each other for about three years before her untimely passing, she made a huge impact on my life. I looked up to her. She was settled. She was soft, loving, and nurturing. Yet she was strong, confident, and independent. She knew where her help came from (the Lord) and she operated in faith. Her trust in God inspired me more than she probably knew. Sadly, I never told her that. It could be I didn't realize how much she inspired me until she was no longer here.

The last time I saw Ms. Bernie was on a Sunday. That would be appropriate. We often saw one another on Sundays. I love a home cooked meal after church on Sundays, in particular. It was hard to cook portions small enough for just my daughter and I so I would frequently share with Ms. Bernie. She was single and lived by herself. She seldom cooked and it blessed me to be able to provide a nice meal for her once in a while.

When she arrived at my house, I was finishing the last of the cooking. She sat at the kitchen table and enjoyed a wonderful conversation with another friend who happened to be visiting as well. The two of them talked and laughed. My heart was so full that day. Like Ms. Bernie, I am a nurturer. It made me feel good to provide a place where the two of them were comfortable, able to relax and enjoy a leisurely afternoon.

Every so often they would reel me into the conversation and it felt like family instead of friends. The warmth, genuine care, ease of conversation, and the eager anticipation of dinner made for an atmosphere of love, respect, and appreciation.

Earlier when Ms. Bernie called, I was in the middle of cleaning the meat I planned to cook for dinner. When I saw her call coming in I thought, "I'll call her later". Please know that was not for any reason of disrespect or an indication I didn't want to talk to her. I simply felt too busy at that moment to stop and answer the phone. I was already feeling a little behind my self-imposed schedule that day.

As soon as her call went to my voicemail something told me to stop what I was doing and call her back. I did. I let her know I was preparing dinner and invited her to stop by. She sounded so happy and grateful for the invitation. Just hearing her voice always calmed me, so the stress I had been feeling about being behind schedule slowly faded away. I don't know what it was about her but she definitely had that gift.

We've all chosen at times not to answer an incoming call because we think we're too busy. Let me tell you, you are not! The meal we shared that day, the laughter, the love, the conversation, the guidance given, the memories made, all of it would be the last I would ever share with her. Ms. Bernie was killed by a drunk driver the following week.

I thank God for the nudging of the Holy Spirit; you know, that 'something' I mentioned earlier. Do you see what I would have been left with had I not answered the call? Guilt, regret, and probably shame. Do you also see what God blessed me with instead? Love; He gave me and my friend one last opportunity to love on her and have her love on us. God knew what was on the horizon but there was no way we could have known.

I'm so glad I listened and called her back. My advice to you is to answer the call; you never know if it will be the last one you will receive from that person.

Day 10 - Moment of Reflection:

Has God given you multiple opportunities to stop and hear Him through circumstances?

_____

_____

_____

_____

_____

_____

_____

_____

_____

_____

_____

_____

_____

_____

_____

_____

_____

_____

_____

Day 11

Facebook

Social media has provided a platform for any and everyone with access to the internet to promote whatever they choose. I choose to be positive and uplifting and like to keep my network the same. Even with social media, I am learning to listen to what the Spirit of the Lord is guiding me to do and say.

There are times I sense so strongly in my spirit that I should write something but question myself if I should post it or not. Generally, it is because I don't understand what it means. That causes me to hesitate.

Despite the hesitation, more than ninety percent of the time I proceed and post it anyway. One of those hesitation posts ended up giving someone a much need shout of victory and breakthrough they were seeking. When we spoke about it over the phone, I could hear the deliverance in his voice. It was amazing! All I could do was say, "Okay, Lord. I see now!"

The post that blessed him and released him from condemnation was this:

Let the redeemed of the Lord say "SO"!!! Oh, you heard I did XYZ back in the day? I may have. Oh, you heard I did ABC at one time? It's quite possible. But what do you know (or think you know) about me now?

The Redeemer lives and I'm so glad about it. I am not who I used to be and I thank God for that. I say "SO" every time the enemy tries to remind me of what "was", because God and I know what "is"!! Trust and believe, I say it with much attitude too because if He has forgiven me, that's ALL that matters!!!

Just a little something the Lord dropped in my spirit to post today. #stayingobedient

True testimonies come with transparency so I can tell you this. There have been times the hesitation was caused by nothing more than fear of perception. At times, I have been more concerned about perception than obedience to God. I guess I didn't want people to think what I wrote pertained to my life and what I may be going through, especially if it didn't. This was the reason the post which blessed a friend almost did not make it to social media. I wasn't going through anything related to what the post spoke of but felt it gave the impression I was dealing with something along those lines.

I'm learning to let go of 'self' a little more with every whisper from the Lord. Everything God speaks to us is not necessarily about us or for us. However, He may want it to come from us for someone else. Had I not been obedient, the person who read that particular post may not have received his breakthrough. Yes, a well-placed post on Facebook, directed by God, can be exactly the thing a person has been waiting for and desperately in need of to move out of their dark place!

If we are going to be used to the fullest for Kingdom purposes, we have to let go of 'self'.

It's not always part of God's plan for us to know the extent to which He is using something so seemingly simple to bless a person in a big way. I am grateful I was permitted to know the end result this time!

I'm still striving to get to the point where I don't hesitate or question the leading, and just roll with it. There are blessings in our obedience. Let us not block someone's blessing, or even our own, by being disobedient.

We should not undervalue the small assignments God gives us. Listen. Obey. The little assignments can prove to be as valuable as those people deem more significant. God knows what His people need and He is faithful to provide from them. He can use our words (both spoken and written) to bring healing, deliverance, and long-sought breakthrough. Be a willing vessel. Be receptive

71

to allowing God to use any method He chooses…even a simple Facebook post!

If my act of obedience blesses just one person it's worth it. The post gave my friend breakthrough and victory over condemnation. His breakthrough is worth much more than any uneasiness I could ever feel in making a simple social media post!

Day 11 - Moment of Reflection:

Are you willing to accept small Kingdom assignments even if they make you uncomfortable?

_____

_____

_____

_____

_____

_____

_____

_____

_____

_____

_____

_____

_____

_____

_____

_____

Day 12
Distraught

One of the hardest things about my style of writing is its personal nature. I write from revelation giving to me through life experiences. Many of these experiences are quite personal. However, there is no way to share the impact of the revelation without being very transparent. That's uncomfortable for me. My desire to help people see God's hand in their daily lives trumps that, however.

When we are in tune with the Holy Spirit, we will do, or not do, things which we may not understand at the moment. In some instances, we may never know why we were led to do or not do a particular thing. Regardless, the key is to be obedient. The Holy Spirit will not lead us to anything damaging or harmful; quite the opposite. He leads and guides to make our lives better, easier, safer, and more peaceful.

When He leads us, the root reason may actually be for someone else's benefit more so than our own. There was an occurrence once which made that point crystal clear for me.

One evening I went to visit a man I had been dating. We watched a movie at his house and then I left. As usual, he walked me to my car which was parked on the street in front of his home. Sitting in front of his neighbor's house, I noticed a car with its parking lights on. It was a little after 10 pm; therefore, it was dark outside. Although I noticed the car and made a joke with him about it, neither one of us paid it much attention. By the time we reached my vehicle, the car was forgotten about.

Once we reach my car, I typically would get in, put my purse down on the passenger seat, start the car, and then get back out for a minute. We would hug one last time and he'd give me a kiss; a quick peck on the lips. I would then get back in the car and leave. This was the norm. There was never anything overly affectionate, and certainly not inappropriate, in our farewell routine but it was very endearing.

Somehow, that night, I knew in my spirit I was not to get back out of the car. The feeling wasn't one of fear. There was nothing to be afraid of. Yet, I knew I wasn't supposed to do it. Instantly I found myself wondering why I wasn't comfortable doing what we always did. It's amazing how many thoughts can run through our minds in a millisecond! I recall thinking, "But I want my hug." None the less, instead of getting back out, I simply looked up at him as he stood by my door and I said goodnight.

He closed my door and started walking back up his driveway. I put my seatbelt on and drove off. As I drove down the street, the car in front of his neighbor's house turned its headlights on and came down the street behind me. I was aware but not worried by any means. However, as I neared the stop sign at the end of the street, the driver of the car behind me flashed the headlights. Now I was a little concerned.

At the stop sign, the driver of that car pulled up on the driver's side of my car and rolled the window down. The driver was an extremely distraught woman.

As it turns out, this was an ex-girlfriend of his from a couple of years prior. She stated very clearly that she was trying to get over him but was having a hard time doing so. She apologized for, in essence, stalking him/us. My heart absolutely broke for her! As soon as the shock of the situation wore off, I understood what the hesitation earlier was about. The Lord loves her, too. He spared her from seeing any display of affection because she would not have been able to handle it at that moment. From what I saw at the stop sign, any affection between him and I would have been the utmost of detrimental for her to witness.

I am so glad I listened to the leading of the Holy Spirit that night. Although she had no right being there, I saw her as a hurting soul. I

never want to add to another person's pain,
even if unknowingly.

Day 12 - Moment of Reflection:

Would you be willing to deny self-satisfaction in order to spare hurt to someone else?

_____

_____

_____

_____

_____

_____

_____

_____

_____

_____

_____

_____

_____

_____

_____

_____

_____

_____

Day 13
Simple
Obedience

Driving to church one Sunday morning, I heard the Spirit of the Lord give me a directive. He told me to call a particular lady and deliver a short message. He told me exactly what I was to say to her. There was no mistaking what I was supposed to do.

The problem I had was, outside of social media, I had never met her before. I didn't know her personally, and she likely knew less of who I was. Would she think I was some crazy chick for reaching out and telling her what God said? The struggle was real. I wanted to be obedient. At the same time, however, I didn't want to come off as strange.

As I drove the rest of the way to church, I tussled with what to do. This was boiling down to a simple matter of obedience; do it and be obedient or don't do it and be disobedient. I was quite aware that if I chose to not deliver the message it would be a willful act of disobedience. I wasn't ready to accept that for a couple of reasons. First, I did not want to purposefully disappoint God. Secondly, I wasn't sure if there would be negative consequences for not doing what I was asked to do. I'm not implying I felt God would punish me if I didn't deliver the message because that is not the case. There are blessings in obedience. I didn't want to miss mine or be the cause of her missing hers.

I decided that as soon as I reached the church, I would send her an inbox message and ask her to call me. In the message, I didn't reference the subject matter for fear she really would think I was nuts. Imagine getting a message from someone who is nothing more than a social media acquaintance which says "Please call me. I have a message for you from God." Really? Would YOU call after getting a message like that? Instead, the message I left in her inbox was generic and simply requested she call me. She is an entrepreneur, so even though we don't know one another, it is possible she may have thought I was reaching out for business reasons.

Later in the day, she called. Regardless of the fact I knew what I was supposed to tell her, I was a bit uncomfortable. Fighting fear made me nervous at best. I was certain of what needed to be said but still felt a little fearful that I would embarrass myself with a stranger. None the less, I took a deep breath and delivered the message.

It never ceases to amaze me what can happen if we remain obedient. Not only did she NOT think I was crazy, she told me just how much she needed to hear those particular words at that moment! Do you see how good God is? He gave her what she needed when she needed it! We can't afford to hesitate when He speaks; someone is depending on us. What He spoke to me was for her at the time He knew she needed it.

I'm sure God could have easily chosen to use her husband, or a host of other people close to her, to deliver the message. I can only guess that He wanted it to come from someone outside of her immediate circle for a specific reason. When encouraging my daughter, she has often told me, "But mommy, you're supposed to say that. You're my mom." From my heart, I am telling my daughter what I genuinely feel. Yet, she discounts it slightly because of who I am to her. Maybe this is the reason God had me speak the message to my social media acquaintance instead of someone closer to her.

God's thoughts and His ways are so much higher than our own (Isaiah 55:9). Therefore it would do no good to spend time pondering the 'whys' of His chosen delivery method. Nor should we spend too much time pondering 'if' we should obey. There are blessings in obedience. Above that, I'm sure it pleases God when we are obedient. After all, we are His children, right? Just as it pleases parents when their children obey their requests, it must please God in the same manner.

Although I did as I was asked that day, there have been days similar situations were presented and the outcome was different. One would think being obedient gets easier after receiving such awesome confirmation but that's not necessarily true. We have to continually fight the spirit of doubt. Okay, I have to continually fight the spirit of doubt. Let me not put that on you!

My desire is to be consistently obedient... regardless! Do it afraid, is a phrase that sums it up best. Otherwise, it can cause us, and others because of us, to miss blessings.

I let fear of looking foolish cause me to be disobedient one day. It was a very similar situation as with the social media friend. The only difference is I knew this person more personally; not well, but personally. We had become friends through a mutual friend. Our friendship is relatively young but we've attended events together several times and have mutual respect and appreciation for one another.

Early one morning, the Holy Spirit told me to call her and let her know she is loved. The

84

conversation which ensued went something like this:

Me: But Lord, she knows she's loved.

Him: Call and tell her she is loved.

Me: But Lord, she has so many other friends much closer to her than I. She'd probably appreciate hearing it from them more than from me.

Him: Call and tell her she is loved.

When God uses words, I always chuckle when I realize how He speaks to me. His words never change. He doesn't try to rephrase, He simply reiterates. I guess it's kind of like God talking to Jonah, telling him to go to Nineveh (Jonah 1: 2 & 3:2). He repeated Himself to Jonah, yet spoke the same words!

Sadly, on this occasion, I must admit I stopped talking to Him after His last reiteration. It wasn't that I didn't want to deliver the message; I was battling fear again. There probably was no good cause for me to hesitate that morning, but I did. Even I couldn't understand why. It is not uncommon for me to randomly reach out to friends, family members, and acquaintances to let them know they are being thought of, are appreciated, and loved. In fact, I'm certain this particular new friend has been the recipient of one of my random messages from time to time. It gives me great joy to surprise people with kind, sincere, and unexpected words. Who doesn't feel good when they know people are thinking of them and wishing them well?

I should have pushed beyond the fear of looking foolish that morning but did not. I went on with my day, giving no further thought to what I had been asked to do… until. Later that afternoon I saw a post she made on social media that she was feeling heartbroken. Her ex-husband passed that day!

The details of their relationship are unclear to me. However, from the post, it was evident she still cared deeply for him and his passing impacted her greatly.

I had no way of knowing she would suffer the loss of a loved one that day. God knows all things though. This is most likely why He asked me to deliver that particular message to her. Can you imagine how disappointed I was in myself once I saw the full picture? Don't wait until you understand the fullness of God's plan to jump on board. Even if it doesn't make sense to you, just do it! It must make perfect sense to Him otherwise He wouldn't have said it. Be obedient at every step along the way.

Obedience to God is the only thing we should concern ourselves with.

We are called to be peculiar people (2 Peter 2:9). The Holy Spirit will lead us to do things which may seem out of the norm, different from others, and that others may not understand. But, there are reasons and generally very good reasons! There are blessings in obedience. Don't miss yours and please do not be the reason someone misses theirs either.

Once I saw her post, I reached out to offer my condolences. I also shared with her what I was led to say that morning but hadn't. I was honest and told her I hesitated because I thought she may think me to be strange. She laughed and assured me she would not have.

The two stories shared are not only examples of obedience. They have served as personal confirmation for me of who God is grooming me to be; an encourager. To be who God is calling me to be, I must stay focused on what I know and not what I feel or fear. I know God is a loving God. If He is asking me to do or say something, it is intended to benefit someone or a situation.

Getting tangled up in our feelings will hinder our growth and God's ability to use us for His purposes.

Day 13 - Moment of Reflection:

What do you have to press beyond in order to be who God is calling you to be?

_____

_____

_____

_____

_____

_____

_____

_____

_____

_____

_____

_____

_____

_____

_____

_____

_____

_____

_____

Day 14

Rags to

Riches

Learning to listen encompasses understanding what has been spoken. Not everything God speaks to us will require action on our part; sometimes just simple acceptance.

In 2015 I was blessed to attend a large, international women's conference. During one of the Saturday worship sessions, the Lord said to me, "You are a rags to riches story". Bear with me as I explain.

When people hear the phrase "rags to riches", the natural inclination is to think financially poor to rich. We see stories about athletes, performers, actors, entrepreneurs, etc. who have gone from low-income childhoods to being mega millionaire adults. Financially rich was not, by far, what God meant in my case. A person can also be spiritually poor or rich; poor or rich in integrity; poor or rich in morals and values. Poor and rich do not necessarily relate to money.

Before I dedicated my life to Christ and was serious about living His way, I was poor in many ways. The core of me has always been a good person, but good people don't always do good things or always have good intentions. I would cut corners to get my way. Spoiled and selfish surely are words that could have been used to describe me. Generous and helpful have been consistent qualities of my personality through life and I'm grateful for that. They balanced out my other not so complimentary qualities.

"You are a rags to riches story" were some of the most significant words spoken to me! When I heard the words, I understood what they meant. Not once did I think, "Okay, the money is coming soon. God said I'm a rags to riches story. The money must be close."

None of that crossed my mind. God was letting me know He sees the change in me. No more lies; no hate; no envy. In their place, He sees truth, joy, peace, pure intentions, and love.

He also knew I needed to know He sees the change in me! To become different (more Christ-like than worldly) there has to be an honest self-evaluation first. The evaluation I did long ago was not very flattering. It yielded much regret and took quite a while to forgive myself for. In fact, the self-evaluation had been painful. The lack of forgiveness weighed heavily on me. All of that was in the past, which is where I needed to leave it. It seemed, however, I was having a difficult time doing that until He spoke those words.

To hear God tell me I've gone from rags to riches blessed my heart in ways I'll never be able to explain. I was still condemning myself for things I did and regretting the circumstances that were created as a result of my bad choices. But the blessing is that God does not hold them against me. That being the case, why should I continue to do so? He sees me as rich; rich in righteousness, rich in peace, rich in understanding, rich in forgiveness, rich in gentleness, rich in generosity, rich in kindness, rich in encouragement. The rags are gone - buried with no visible grave markers. He doesn't want me, or YOU, to walk around with a sad or shameful countenance (grave markers) because of things we did. What is important is what we do now and who we are now. That's all that matters. 2 Corinthians 5:17 "If any man be in Christ he is a new creature, old things are passed away, behold, all things become new."

God speaking to me was amazing enough by itself. However, He gave me a sense of validation I longed for. I desired to know my ways pleased Him. To realize He sees me as a "rags to riches story" was monumental! And if God viewed me that way, it was certainly time I began seeing myself that way as well; regardless of the mistakes I had made in life. I believe this to be the reason He shared His view with me. Had he not, I may still be struggling to see my value in Him.

Let the redeemed of the Lord say SO! We don't have to be held responsible all the days of our lives for what we did or who we were.

We've been redeemed. If the only person available to remind you of that is you, remind yourself as often as needed. It is so important to do so or you may remain stuck in guilt and regret.

I once heard a pastor say, "It's easy to tell on yourself when that's not who you are anymore." I don't share these personal things about myself for any purpose other than to give God glory for what He has done in my life. While I yet have a long way to go, I thank God for speaking to me that Saturday morning and telling me how He sees me, which is how I should see myself.

Day 14 - Moment of Reflection:

What has God spoken to you about your walk
with Him, and do you understand what He
means?

_____

_____

_____

_____

_____

_____

_____

_____

_____

_____

_____

_____

_____

_____

_____

_____

_____

Day 15

ESP is a
God Thing

Such a cute God-thing happened one day at work. Before leaving home, I decided to pack a lunch for myself. While making mine, I felt led to make another plate for a co-worker. This woman is by no means in need. Because of that, I started questioning myself: "Do I need to take food for her. She didn't ask me to bring lunch for her. Will she be offended and think I perceive her as a person in need? I'm really not that great of a cook. She may not even like what I bring." Although the doubt persisted I ignored it and packed lunch for her as well.

Soon after arriving at work, I called her desk. When I told her I had lunch for her she said, "How did you know I didn't have anything for lunch? I was going to tell you if you go out for lunch today to please bring me back something! You must have ESP!"

Well folks, I think I do have ESP...Extra Sensitivity to the Power and leading of the Holy Spirit! I had no idea why she crossed my mind that morning. Bringing lunch for her was not a habit or anything I could recall doing before that day. But on that day I was led to. My obedience to the leading of the Holy Spirit resulted in an on-time blessing for her! Many times I have said, "There are blessings in obedience". Little blessings count as much as big blessings, so no matter how small or random the act of kindness may seem to be, do it! The Holy Spirit will never lead you wrong.

Even if she had said, "Thanks but I brought lunch today", I would have been okay. I was obedient to His leading. Had she declined the food I would have looked at it as a small test of obedience. If we are faithful with the small things, God knows He can trust us with bigger things (tasks, Kingdom assignments).

What I was asked to do that morning seemed quite random to me. However, it wasn't random at all. God knew from the beginning of time that she would appreciate having lunch brought to her that specific day. It may seem like an overly spiritual way to look at the events of that morning it but it is indeed a true statement.

Day 15 - Moment of Reflection:

Can you think of a time you talked yourself out of doing a small, seemingly random, act of kindness for someone because you didn't understand why you were doing it?

_____

_____

_____

_____

_____

_____

_____

_____

_____

_____

_____

_____

_____

_____

_____

_____

_____

Day 16
A Walk
With God

While at work one afternoon, I decided to take a break. There is a nice park very close to my job so I went there. The setting of the park is very serene and I had begun taking frequent walks there. More often than not the walks became prayer time. This day, in particular, I remember asking God to speak to me because I was listening. In hindsight, I can't recall dealing with anything specific I wanted to hear from Him about. I just wanted Him to talk to me. I didn't have a prayer request so I thanked Him for being who He is to me and then waited as I walked.

The sidewalk goes all the way around the entire park. Therefore I start and end in the same location. On the way back I felt the Holy Spirit tell me to spin around in a circle. That seemed like such a bizarre request to me. I wasn't listening to music, so if I did do as I was being asked to do it wasn't as if I could pass it off as a fancy dance move or anything. None the less, I was obedient. I extended both of my arms out wide on each side of my body and as I took my next step, I spun in one complete circle. As soon as I came out of the spin I put my arms down at my sides and kept walking forward. I didn't miss a beat!

I was amused by this little episode because I sensed God was testing me. I asked Him to speak and He did. Could it be He wanted to see if I was really listening by giving me a little test? Additionally, would I obey because it was something silly? Being silly for God privately is one thing. Following His lead and looking foolish publically is another. What God says won't always make sense to us in the natural but it's important to follow through. We cannot put more importance on what people think of us than what God is asking us to do.

When things like that happen I believe they are preludes of things to come. Would there soon come a time when God would have me to do something a little bigger and more important than spin in a circle? Would I hesitate if I did not understand the reason He was asking me to do it? I prayed that day that I would not. The test I was given that day has allowed me to remain aware that I should be ready to act when He speaks.

Listening to God does no good if we're not willing to be obedient to Him. Hearing and doing are two different things. This is why the word of God tells us we have to be "doers of the word, and not hearers only" (James 1:22). And yes, there may come a time when being obedient may cause us to look foolish. It's all about trust. Can He trust us to follow His lead? It is important to understand God will never speak and ask us to do anything which may place us in harm's way. Our trust and faith in Him may cause us to look foolish to others at times but trusting God and having faith in Him will not lead to harm.

He may tell you to apply for a job you are not qualified for. Others will think you're foolish for submitting the application. I love stories of motivational speakers who struggled with speech impediments as children but go on to become great speakers. People around them likely thought they were foolish for pursuing such a career. What they may not know is God gave them the green light and told them if they were obedient and followed His lead, He would make sure every word spoken out of their mouths were completely understood!

Day 16 - Moment of Reflection:

Do you trust God enough to look foolish for Him?

_____

_____

_____

_____

_____

_____

_____

_____

_____

_____

_____

_____

_____

_____

_____

_____

_____

_____

_____

Day 17

Thy Right Hand

At a retreat one year, I had an incredible encounter with God. He held my hand! I say this in the most tangible way possible because I could feel the pressure of His hand on mine. I have felt His Spirit around me on many occasions. However, it was always a spiritual presence. This was the only time in my life I have physically felt His presence.

My belief is that God does all things with intention. As such, as soon as I was able to move from the sheer awe of the moment, I immediately began to wonder the significance of Him holding my left hand. I asked a couple of people, who I deemed a bit more Biblically knowledgeable, if they were aware of the significance of God holding my left hand. No one had an answer.

As time went on, I concerned myself less with the matter of the left hand and simply focused on the fact God manifested Himself to me in such a marvelous way. Leave it to me to get caught up in the 'why'.

Two years later while reading the book of Psalm I stumbled on the answer. I was looking for something completely unrelated to the hand-holding incident when I found myself focusing in on Psalms 138:7. After reading it, I realized my two-year-old question had indeed been answered.

Psalm 138:7 Though I walk in the midst of trouble, thou will revive me: thou shall stretch forth thine hand against the wrath of my enemies, and THY RIGHT HAND shall save me.

It was never about my left hand, but His right hand! For all I had been through, and for all

He knew was still to come, He loved me enough to let me know He shall save me!

There are a few lessons I was able to gain from the overall experience:

Lesson 1: It's not always about us. My mind could only compute that God held my left hand. Standing beside me as He was, it was His right hand holding my left. That was the key factor.

Lesson 2: Often times we seek man for answers when the Bible answers every question we could possibly have.

Lesson 3: Sometimes we may have to wait for understanding to come. Listening requires patience. I always knew there was a reason He held my hand. I was just misguided in thinking it was about my left hand when it was all about His mighty right hand. It took two years for the significance of the moment to be made clear to me.

Day 17 - Moment of Reflection:

Have you ever silently wondered about, prayed for, and asked others to help you understand something only to eventually find it was available to you all along in the Bible?

_____

_____

_____

_____

_____

_____

_____

_____

_____

_____

_____

_____

_____

_____

_____

_____

Day 18

Breathing

Easy

"Breathing easy"; that's what God spoke to me the day after my mother passed. Specifically, His words were, "She's breathing easy now."

It was a small statement. It required no action on my part. His words were designed to give me the peace I needed to handle losing her. Next to losing a child, I believe the loss of a parent is the most painful reality we can experience in life. The depth of sorrow knows no boundaries. The length of the mourning seemingly has no end. And, the physical pains I experienced were unexpected.

When my mother passed, my heart physically hurt. I never knew that type of physical pain was possible. Some wondered if I meant emotional pain. I did not. While I was emotionally distraught, the physical pain in my heart was another matter. All along I knew the physical agony was not a precursor to a heart attack. This anguish was tied to my soul which had been all but ripped out of my body.

Sometimes when God speaks it is to give us direction on what to do, what not to do; where to go, where not to go; who to build relationships with or who to cut ties with. Then there are times He speaks simply to comfort us. I desperately needed comfort when I woke up that morning. God was faithful to His very nature and provided it. Knowing my mother was breathing easy shifted something in me which I cannot explain. It made everything okay. It didn't take the pain or sadness away but it surely dulled it some. As the days passed by, it became well with my soul. Not only was my mother no longer struggling to breathe, but God also said she was breathing EASY now!

The Bible tells us that the Lord is close to the brokenhearted (Psalms 34:18). He surely had to have been close to me from the moment I found out my mother passed, through her home-going service, and even to today. Nothing will ever change the fact that I miss her, long to talk with her, give her a hug, and send her a birthday card or a Christmas present. But, being without her is well with my soul because God reassured me that she's okay.

Learning to listen and discern the voice of God involves knowing who God is. If we do not know the fullness of what He is capable of being to and for us, we can easily miss what He is trying to do.

In this particular case, Jehovah Shalom, the God of peace, was with me. Had it not been for the peace He so graciously gave through the words spoken, I doubt the days, weeks, months, and possibly years after losing my mother would have been as tolerable. If I did not know He was able to provide peace, it is likely I may not have accepted what He said that morning.

What if I had dismissed what I heard by say, "Breathing easy, what does that mean? Who is breathing easy? My Mother is not breathing easy because she's gone!" Had I remained stuck in my pain and sorrow, instead of receiving the peace and comfort which was so graciously being offered to me, where would I be today? Still hurting, Heaven forbid!

Day 18 - Moment of Reflection:

Through the years, what has God been to you?

_____

_____

_____

_____

_____

_____

_____

_____

_____

_____

_____

_____

_____

_____

_____

_____

_____

_____

Day 19
Broken

A dear friend of mine once said, "You can see a bug on a leaf and find spiritual significance in it." That may be so, since this particular short story isn't too far of a case scenario from her statement.

While at the beach one beautiful Florida afternoon, a friend and I were collecting seashells. She picked up a couple of broken shells and asked if I wanted them. I told her no because I only wanted the whole ones. We enjoyed the rest of our beach time and continued on with our search; me, looking for whole shells, and her looking for whichever ones she saw beauty in. Although I could not see beauty in the broken ones, she could.

A little while later God reminded me of something I will never again forget. He reminded me that He accepted me despite my brokenness. As a matter of fact, He accepted me because of my brokenness. When I came to Him and accepted Him as my Lord and Savior, I stood before Him broken, knowing that I needed Him. In my weakest, most broken state, He wanted me. How dare I not see the beauty in their brokenness when God saw mine?

God sees the beauty in us despite our brokenness and He accepts us just as we are. His loving reminder at the beach helped me see beauty everywhere and in everyone. Granted, when it comes to people, it can be a little harder, but it is possible. Learning how to accept difficult or mean-spirited people despite their brokenness is no easy task but they are souls just like the rest of us. Souls worth saving.

When we listen to God's voice, we gain wisdom. Whether it is the rain, the snow, the thick of the fog, or broken shells, there is beauty because there is purpose! As a matter of fact, someone close to me, a few years after the seashell incident and with no knowledge of it, said to me, "You live life as if you once died and came back to life. You see beauty in everything." How can I not? God made everything and everything He made is good!

"Broken crayons still color"; I do not know the origin of that phrase but I love it. Broken crayons can still color which means they can still serve a purpose. Some of us are broken but that does not mean we cannot and should not live a purpose driven life!

Day 19 - Moment of Reflection:

Has there been a time you may have thought less of something or someone because of the incomplete condition you perceived them to be in?

_____

_____

_____

_____

_____

_____

_____

_____

_____

_____

_____

_____

_____

_____

Day 20
Not Today
Devil

As with most mothers and teen daughters, I went through a period of time when things were very challenging with mine. Our relationship had been somewhat strained and I wasn't happy about it. I wanted our closeness back. I wanted to go and enjoy outings with her as we used to do. One day she gave me a glimmer of hope. She asked if I would take her to the Holy Land Experience in Orlando. To say that I was excited would be a gross understatement. I had recently visited the Holy Land Experience and found it to be very spiritually moving. When my daughter asked to go I jumped at the

118

opportunity to take her and share in such an experience with her.

The day came and we were both excited about going. We arrived just before they opened so we could experience everything they had to offer on the schedule.

Soon after we arrived, my daughter said she was hungry. We went to the café to get lunch. We sat outside enjoying the food, the view, and each other. Our day was off to such a fabulous start!

After eating a couple of bites of my food, I could tell I had eaten something I am allergic to. My mouth started itching and the skin on the roof of my mouth felt tight which meant it was swelling up. These are typical symptoms of an allergic reaction for me. Having experienced this too many times to count, I knew it meant a trip to the emergency room. That would then mean my daughter and I would miss out on the Holy Land Experience together. I was not willing to do that, despite what was happening! There was no way I was going to let the devil steal our day. It was too important and significant.

You may wonder why I automatically accused the devil. He had been fighting my daughter tooth and nail for a long time, keeping her away from anything Christ-like. Once she made up in her mind she was going to the Holy Land, he realized his next best bet to keep her from that would be to get to me. Since I would never tell her that I wouldn't take her, the only thing he could do was find a way to bring our day to an abrupt end. Oh, but God!

God loves us so much He has given us the means to fight back! I'm grateful I was able to remember it at that moment.

I pushed my food to the side, looked at my daughter and said, "Something is not right with my food but I am NOT having an allergic reaction and I need you to agree with me on that. I rebuke this in the name of Jesus". She verbally agreed with me by repeating my statement to include the words "in the name of Jesus". She then shared her food with me. Within a matter of two minutes, every symptom I had been having was gone! The itching had stopped, the swelling in my mouth had gone down, and my throat felt fine. Never before had a reaction stopped in its tracks, especially without medication and professional treatment, but God did it!

Luke 10:19 reminds us that God has given us power to trample on the head of the enemy, and nothing shall by any means hurt you. The power referred to is the name of Jesus. At the name of Jesus, everything must bow. Please remember that in your time of need, regardless of the situation.

The last event we attended that day at the Holy Land Experience was precisely what the enemy had been trying to keep my daughter away from. She was blessed and deeply touched by the service. It was more than a performance; it was a church service with a profoundly moving illustrated sermon and the presence of the Lord was there!

The focus of this book is learning to listen. Are you wondering yet what God spoke to me on this day? Have you gone back and scanned the words to see what He told me that I listened to? You may very well be trying

121

to figure out what this particular story has to do with learning to listen.

I believe learning to listen involves applying what we've already learned/heard. I knew what the word of God said in Luke 10:19. I had previously heard it, I believed it to be true, and I applied it. God said we could and I believed Him.

By definition, learning means "to gain or acquire knowledge of". What is the benefit of gaining the knowledge if we don't apply it?

Day 20 - Moment of Reflection:

Do you recall a time the enemy tried to keep you from something you knew was meant for your good? How did you handle it?

_____

_____

_____

_____

_____

_____

_____

_____

_____

_____

_____

_____

_____

_____

_____

_____

_____

Day 21

The Message Was Still Valid

There was a day at work when I clearly heard the Lord leading me to deliver a word from Him to a co-worker. By no means do I consider myself a prophet but I know what the Lord told me to do and say. I'll admit and tell you that I was hesitant. Certainly, I am not ashamed of my relationship with Christ so that was not a factor in my hesitation. What it boiled down to was, to the best of my remembrance, this was the first time God had used me in this manner. This was new for me. Anything new can easily take us out of our comfort zone. God was surely stretching me outside of mine with this assignment.

124

Although I knew full well what I was being directed to do that day, I didn't do it. I gave myself every excuse: "He's busy working", "He'll think I'm crazy for saying this", etc. The sad part is that I could see on his face that he was struggling with something. Yet, I remained disobedient to the leading of the Spirit.

I went home that evening very disappointed in myself. By this point in my life, I had become well aware there are blessings in obedience. Therefore, I understood I was potentially depriving either my co-worker or myself (or possibly both of us) of a blessing by not being obedient. As a result, I could not rest well at all that night. I promised God and myself when I got to work the next day, I would do as I knew I should have the day before; deliver the message.

Early the next morning I saw my co-worker outside the building. Although I still had butterflies in my stomach, I was determined to overcome them. When I approached him we began a regular conversation. At the moment I sensed the timing was right, I shifted gears in the conversation and let him

125

know I had something to share with him. I'm not sure I needed to give him the background on what I had gone through the day before, but I did. Maybe I was supposed to as encouragement for him to listen and obey God without hesitation as well. Whether or not he needed the background story, he seemed to appreciate my honesty.

As I began telling him what God told me, he stood there in silence. I wasn't sure how to take his silence and tried not to focus on it. My concern was delivering the message I was asked to deliver and I had.

When I finished speaking, he thanked me and said he needed to hear that. He shared some of his struggles with me and indicated he was sure the message was from God and meant for him because what I told him his Grandmother had as well. What a relief! I was relieved the message was still valid and not just for the day I didn't deliver it.

We are not always guaranteed to have the opportunity to correct ourselves the next day.

Therefore, I encourage you, no matter how new, how difficult, or how uncomfortable, act on God's words when He speaks them.

Day 21 - Moment of Reflection:

What are some of the reasons you hesitate in being obedient?

_____

_____

_____

_____

_____

_____

_____

_____

_____

_____

_____

_____

_____

_____

_____

_____

_____

_____

Day 22

The

Word

While in the process of compiling stories to include in this book, I had the opportunity to talk with someone who had purchased the first one. He asked if we could talk very specifically about one particular subject regarding it. He wanted to know how I hear from God. His desire to know for sure that he is hearing from God was so heartwarming. The question led to such a wonderful conversation which I was honored to be part of.

As we talked, I let him in a little secret. I gave him some of the insight being shared in this book. It was refreshing to have such a dialogue. He was genuinely seeking a deeper relationship with Christ and any guidance I could give was a privilege.

The gentleman wanted to know how I developed a connection with God to the point where I am sure it is Him speaking to me. As I shared the ways I've learned God speaks, he listened intently. The opportunities God has given me to share more about Him have been quite moving. This exchange was one of those moving moments.

After our conversation, the Holy Spirit revealed another form of communication to me: the Word. Yes, the Bible and its contents. I've always known that the Word of God was written to speak His commandments and desires for our lives. The revelation I received after the discussion with this gentleman was beyond that level of knowledge.

There are times when the Word of God (scripture) will drop into my spirit seemingly out of nowhere. Right in the middle of a conversation or situation I am trying to work my way through, I will hear a scripture. That's

God speaking. When this happens, He is guiding us with His Word to help us make the best decisions and choices possible. It will always be up to us whether or not to listen. Are we willing to comply with what we hear?

Although not impossible, it is highly uncommon for God to speak to us in this way if we don't already know scripture. There has to be a level of familiarity with the Word in order for God to bring it back to our remembrance. This is different than making a conscientious effort to recall and recite the Word in times of need. These are not the "The Lord is my shepherd, I shall not want" type of scripture recollection moments in times of distress. What I'm referring to here are the occasions we may not even realize it would be prudent to pause and apply scripture to our situation. Therefore, when He places one in our spirit it may seem random and unexpected but rest assured, it is purposeful. Exercise wisdom in those situations. Quiet yourself enough to discern its intended application to your life and the situation at hand.

For example: While working through a relationship concern years ago, the Holy Spirit kept reminding me of Amos 3:3, which, in summary, asks "How can two people walk together except they agree?" Had I not been familiar with that verse in the Bible, how could God give it back to me in the time I needed to apply it to that relationship? This gentleman I was dating was of a different religious belief than me. Reminding me of that scripture was a form of speaking. As such, God was giving me guidance to help make the best decision possible for my life.

Here is another example. None of us can go through life without having a difference of opinion or even disagreements with others from time to time. I recall one of those instances. It seemed the only thing a particular individual wanted to do was live in strife. I couldn't understand it and was quite frustrated by it. On more than one occasion I heard Romans 12: 18 "If it be possible, as much as lieth in you, live peaceably with all men." I was not actively scanning my memory bank for an appropriate scripture, it just came to me during the times I was feeling frustrated at the inability to be at peace with this person.

I knew this was God's way of telling me the ball was in my court, so to speak. In order to minimize the strife and tension, He was asking me to do all I could to live in peace with the person. As mentioned previously, the choice is ours but it would be foolish not to heed to the guidance being provided. God will always have our best interest at heart.

I'd like to give clarity to a matter regarding scripture. When I say 'a scripture dropped in my Spirit', it does not mean (for me) that I heard it as "Romans 12:18 If it be possible, as much as lieth in you, live peaceably with all men." I'm not that much of a Bible scholar. What I generally will hear is "If it be possible, as much as lieth in you, live peaceably with all men." More often than not I have to go look up the scripture to recall its location in the Bible. I do not want to mislead anyone into thinking I am a Bible scholar, or that the Lord speaks that specifically to me in these situations. In my defense, however, there are a few times where I will surprise myself and know the book, chapter, and verse!

Attending a church that teaches the Bible (scriptures not just the concepts of them) will allow God an opportunity to talk with you through them.

Day 22 - Moment of Reflection:

Can you recall a time scripture seemed to come to you out of nowhere? Did you know how to apply it to your situation?

_____

_____

_____

_____

_____

_____

_____

_____

_____

_____

_____

_____

_____

_____

_____

_____

_____

_____

_____

_____

Day 23

August: Defining Moments

We all have defining moments in life. One of mine was August 2014. Yes, pretty much the entire month of August that year. In this instance then I suppose it was a defining month, not moment. There were key opportunities that month to make Spirit-based decisions versus decisions driven by the flesh. In hindsight, I am grateful to have made the right choices. Albeit difficult to do, they led to blessings I never would have imagined possible.

2013 was without a shadow of a doubt the hardest year of my life. I suffered greatly and

136

endured plenty, but survived by the grace of God through faith. The entire year of 2014 was spent being grateful to simply be living as a sane, functioning human being. Surviving 2013 created in me a desire to live more intentionally than before. I wanted to make a difference like never before. I wanted to engage in life in ways I never had before. I wanted to live a more purpose-filled life.

There were two things I vowed to do just for myself in 2014; take a trip to Georgia in May and Texas in August. The Georgia trip was solely for the purpose of going somewhere quaint I had never been; somewhere I could relax and enjoy new things. The trip to Texas was to serve two purposes: 1) visit a long-time friend and 2) visit the church of a pastor I had wanted to see in person for years. I was very excited about both trips. Unfortunately, the summer got away from me and I was unable to make it to Georgia. However, I had purchased a plane ticket to Texas so that trip was sure to take place, or so I thought.

As the weeks of the summer passed by and August drew near, I felt a pulling in my spirit to cancel the trip to Texas and stay in Tampa.

A cousin was graduating college, a friend invited me to a women's retreat, and the very pastor I wanted to see in Texas was scheduled to preach at a local church in my area the same weekend I planned to go to his church!

I had promised my friend I was coming to see her and I was truly looking forward to going. The thought of disappointing her bothered me. The fact remained, however, that despite the months of advance planning, I was now losing my desire to go and everything in me was saying "stay".

My dilemma was not simply a matter of me changing my mind and wanting to stay in Tampa. I knew I was supposed to stay. Yet, I was still torn. I knew if the Spirit of the Lord was telling me to stay it was for a very good reason. The hard part was the possibility of disappointing my friend. Both of us had been excited about the weekend for a while. She had previously visited me in Tampa but I had not visited her in Texas. When I called to explain my situation, she completely understood. I appreciated it and now, no longer plagued by guilt, I began looking forward to the weekend in Tampa. Even though I knew God wanted me to stay, I had no idea the fullness of what He had in store for me.

Calling my dear friend was the first defining moment in a series of many. Not succumbing to the obligation of the commitment I had made was huge for me. I certainly do not see my friends as obligations. However, when I make commitments I strive to honor them.

The first activity of the weekend was the start of the women's retreat Friday evening. After pulling into the parking lot of the hotel, I took a picture outside by the water. I recall posting it on social media and saying I was at the conference with a "spirit of expectancy". I said it and I fully meant it but still had no idea what to expect. I had never been to the event before and only vaguely knew a handful of the expected attendees.

On Day 17 I touched on the profound experience I had at the retreat. Here I would like to share the full story of the Lord holding my hand that night.

I had just gone back to my seat, which was at the end of the row, after the altar call. The atmosphere was one of deep worship. The presence of the Lord was so strong, I could not sit. I stood at my seat and continued to worship. Both of my arms were raised, my eyes were closed, and my head slightly bowed. As I stood there worshipping, I felt someone take my left hand into their hand. The group of ladies who were working the event had already shown themselves to be loving and supportive from the moment I walked in the room that evening. I began to wonder which one of them was holding my hand. I assumed one of them saw the emotional experience I had at the altar and was there at my seat with me to offer support and encouragement.

After about a minute, curiosity set in and I wanted to see the lady holding my hand and give her a smile of thanks. I opened my eyes and turned my head to the left prepared to show my appreciation with a thankful smile and then return to worship. The only problem was when I turned to my left and opened my eyes there was no one standing there. I could not see anyone yet I could still feel someone holding/squeezing my hand! I knew then, as I still know today, that it was the Lord! Why He chose to reveal Himself to me in such a physically tangible way I don't fully understand but it meant so much. He confirmed for me as never before that He is with me and that I am His and He loves me. I was so humbled by that. Who am I that He would be mindful enough of me to show up there and hold my hand? Walking in the door that evening I had a spirit of expectancy but never knew I could experience anything like that! It was a defining moment! It opened my eyes to how God sees me. As the days, weeks, months, and years since then have passed, I am learning more and more who I am to Him.

I left the retreat that evening completely in awe of the experience. Words are inadequate to describe or explain what took place inside of me. By Him holding my hand, I believe part of what He was trying to tell me is we were now going to truly do this thing called life together! Our relationship moved to a new plateau.

The next morning I was eager for the second day of activity. Still in amazement at the events the night before, it didn't cross my mind that anything else so miraculous could occur. There were no preconceived thoughts or expectations in my mind. The genuine and welcoming fellowship that took place the night before was drawing me back. The atmosphere set was also the safest place to worship that I've ever been in my entire life. Although I had no major expectations, I wanted to go back to experience more of that.

Shame on me for not having expectations! It felt as if the presence of the Lord never left the room overnight! There came a point in the morning I received prayer. Afterward, I experienced yet another new thing with God. My audible was stuck on one phrase: "Use me, Lord, use me." This was involuntary and uncontrollable. In a soft voice, almost at whisper level, the phrase rolled off my tongue hundreds of times over the next several minutes.

Part of what seemed to be taking place was surrender. For the first time, I sensed I was completely giving myself to God for Him to use me as He sees fit. This, too, was a defining moment. I knew in my heart I was ready and willing to accept His will for my life.

If the story of the weekend ended here, I would have been quite satisfied. But it didn't. Sunday evening a friend and I were blessed to attend the special church service where the pastors from Texas preached. I knew the events of Friday night and Saturday morning could not be topped, no matter how much I admired and respected his anointing. I viewed the opportunity to see him as icing on the cake of what had already become a life-changing weekend. Oh, how sweet that icing turned out to be!

As we entered the sanctuary we realized we hadn't arrived early enough to get good seats. We were not in the back. The seats we were able to find were at the midpoint of the sanctuary but we had hoped to get closer. Although they were not ideal seats, I was so excited to hear him speak that it didn't matter. I also realized the seats we had could have been worse so I was grateful.

Friday I declared the expectation of something good and received it. Saturday I did not make a declaration but experienced great things. No declaration was made Sunday either but the favor of God found us. One of the ushers knew the friend I was with. She moved us forward to the 3rd row from the pulpit. Our seats were now in the direct line of sight of the guest speaker from Texas!

When he took the podium, he preached about breaking routines. His message, in essence, was too many Christians have fallen into complacency with life and are living below God's desire for them. He said, "We get up, get dressed, go to work, go home" and repeated it a few times for emphasis. I couldn't believe it; THAT WAS ME! The pastor had just perfectly described my day-to-day routine. Being three seats away from him, and in direct line of sight, added to the sense he was preaching to me and me alone. The bottom line of the message was about doing things different or new.

The experience of being present for one of his messages was all I knew it would be. I was so spiritually full at this point that I wasn't sure I could hold any more spiritual feeding that weekend! It was yet another defining moment for me. A change was on the horizon and I was absolutely ready to embrace it.

If we pause here and reflect, it is very easy to see why the Lord wanted me to stay in Tampa. He had divine encounters for me that were too important for my life to miss. Had I gone to Texas I would not have been where I needed to be for Him to hold my hand. I would have missed understanding that He desired for our relationship to go higher and deeper.

I can again say, if the story of the weekend ended here I would be satisfied. But it didn't!

At the end of the service, my friend and I stayed in the sanctuary for a while. At one point she attended the church so she saw several people and wanted to say hello to them. During this time of socializing, I met an acquaintance of hers. He would later introduce me to a group of women who would become friends of mine. It is with that group of women I traveled to the large, international women's conference the following year (2015). One of the speakers, whom I affectionately call an Australian dynamo, preached a message that was, in part, about passing the baton of faith to the next generation. Her message was the catalyst I needed to finish writing my first book, *Survival by Faith*.

The Lord promised me that if I were obedient in publishing the book people would be blessed. He kept His promise (of course!). The book has provided hope and encouragement to many. It has helped readers see the hand of God operating in all situations, not just good ones. It has strengthened their faith which has enabled them to continue to stand and know that all will be well!

The ripple effect of saying 'yes' to the Holy Spirit and staying in Tampa August of 2014 goes on from there. This short story does not tell it all, but it at least gives you a pretty good overview of why I had to stay. One obedient 'yes' yielded so much fruit! A great deal of Kingdom purpose was birthed, revealed, and discovered that month through many defining moments.

Day 23 - Moment of Reflection:

Can you see the fruit of a 'yes' you gave God?

_____

_____

_____

_____

_____

_____

_____

_____

_____

_____

_____

_____

_____

_____

_____

_____

_____

_____

_____

_____

Day 24

Ladies Encouraging Ladies

I often refer back to the years 2013-2014. They were turning points in my life. The two year season yielded much pain which led to much purpose.

Many of my days in 2013 were spent in confusion and turmoil, to say the least. Since then, I can recall saying, "The Lord was silent and never spoke a word that year." I've recently been reminded that is not a completely accurate statement. Although He did not answer any of the questions I had that year, there was something He spoke quite clearly to me.

"Ladies Encouraging Ladies". Sometime between February and March of 2013 the Lord spoke those three words into my Spirit. I had no clue what they were to represent. Initially, I took them at face value and applied a very surface meaning to them. During that time period, I was dealing with a major health situation which rendered me physically limited. There were a handful of ladies who took great care of me and kept me encouraged. I was so thankful for them. Had it not been for all of their love, support, and encouragement, I'm not sure how I would have gotten through the first three months of the year.

When the health crisis was over I wanted to thank them. Remembering the words the Lord had spoken, I presented them with awards acknowledging and thanking them for their encouragement. The awards were engraved with those words – Ladies Encouraging Ladies. My simple and limited mind thought this to be the reason the Lord placed those words in my Spirit.

As time passed, I began to sense Ladies Encouraging Ladies was to encompass more than the awards of gratitude given to friends and family members that year. From 2013 until 2018 I sought the Lord diligently for understanding. Despite my seeking, not much was being revealed. Throughout the years, I took it upon myself to apply the words to various situations and endeavors. While the efforts extended certainly blessed others, the label of Ladies Encouraging Ladies didn't seem to fit. The work done was not in vain but I knew I could not place an official label on them.

While in the shower one August morning in 2018, the Lord decided it was time! In the matter of a ten-minute shower, He down-loaded an entire mentorship program and let me know that was what He intended all along as Ladies Encouraging Ladies! He spoke the subject matters, showed me the initial group of young ladies to invite as participants, and went so far as to show me the ladies in my circle who would assist by being presenters! When He's ready, He's ready! I was in absolute awe.

As soon as I got out of the shower I got on the laptop and typed the program out. When I saw with my natural eyes what God had just provided to bless His people, it left me speechless and in tears. A short while after, He encouraged me to find scripture to support the topics to be discussed. Again, I was left blown away.

At the time this portion of the book is being written, we are midway through the first class of the mentorship program. Each young lady as provided heart-warming feedback and each presenter has counted it a blessing to share knowledge and experience with them. The life skills they are obtaining at this stage in their lives are so beneficial. As for me, I sit back in awe and reverence each session as I observe what the Lord has orchestrated.

A seed was planted but it took five years for the harvest to manifest. I don't know all of His reasons for the five-year process; however, I can acknowledge at least two of them. In the period of waiting, God had work to do in me. Additionally, there were connections yet to be made in order for the specific presenters and participants to be a part of the program. The Lord requires we do everything decently and in order (I Corin 14:40). This is the best way to ensure success and full impact. Waiting may be a prerequisite depending upon His desired outcome.

Put a pause on it. If you've heard God speak something to you which you know will require action, resist the urge to force its birth / development. Act on it only when you are sure the time is right. When He speaks, He may simply be planting a seed which must be watered for a while. Harvest time may not be scheduled for days, weeks, or years to come. Don't lose sight of it, however. Feel free to go back to Him in prayer from time to time and inquire. I believe He will appreciate your patient desire to see it come to pass. When it does, be sure to give Him all the glory for it.

The ladies in our mentorship program are quite aware of how Ladies Encouraging Ladies came to be. We acknowledge God and thank Him for giving us the program. How can we not? When the invitations to participate were sent out, one of the young ladies responded by saying, "I've been praying for something like this."

Her reply served as the final piece of confirmation I needed. At that point, I knew beyond any doubt the program is what the Lord had in mind from the beginning. When He provided the outline in August of 2018, I knew I would follow through and launch the program. His words were too clear for me not to. However, I had to fight the enemy which should have been expected. Nothing God gives us to do is without Kingdom building purpose. That makes the devil mad and he will try to sabotage it. I went through a few months of delay before the program was implemented. It could have been done in two weeks since He gave me everything required (topics, presenters, and participants). The delay was a result of self-doubt: "I've never done anything like this before." Well, guess what? I'M STILL NOT DOING IT, God is! He's just doing it through me and He fully equipped me for it.

We are much more useable when we get over ourselves!

Day 24 - Moment of Reflection:

Have you ever known God wanted you to do something, yet it didn't take root when you attempted to do it? Can you see through this experience there may have been a waiting period required for you, too?

Day 25
Stop
Talking

Have you ever sought God's advice or
opinion on something simple? I have. I'll
admit I've even asked Him to show me what
to wear on an occasion or two. As our
relationship with Him grows and deepens, it is
wise of us to seek His input on great and
small matters.

A few years ago, I decided to ask God His
desire for me at the beginning of each New
Year. New Year's resolutions were always
difficult for me to keep so I stopped making
them. However, at the onset of each New

Year, I still felt a need to challenge myself to grow and be better. One of my perennial goals is to grow spiritually. Therefore, it seemed appropriate to ask God for His input regarding that area of my life.

I have a deep desire for people to know there is a living God and He is accessible! We simply have to put ourselves in the correct posture to interact with Him. Scripture is so clear in showing us how to do this. When we seek God, we find Him (Jeremiah 29:13). When we ask, He gives (Matthew 7:7). Regardless of knowing and believing both of these verses, I still found myself a bit in awe each year when He gave me the direction I sought from Him. There was never a doubt that God was able to speak His desire to me. It's simply a surreal and wonderful feeling when He does. Almost too good to be true, but it is!

Through the years, I have found it interesting that the Lord's responses have been brief. He doesn't lecture nor belabor His point. Generally what He says consists of one, two, or three words. The simplicity with which He guides me is greatly appreciated. I may have to seek Him for a complete understanding of some words because they have multiple meanings, but His replies to me are never complex in nature.

For example, one year the guidance I received was "light and bold". This was a time I needed to delve deeper. The word light, for instance, can mean a couple of different things. Before I could apply God's guidance to my life that year, I had to seek Him to be sure I understood His specific intent with the word 'light'. Was He asking me to be more of a light for people to see Him (Matthew 5:16…Let your light so shine)? Was He instructing me to be more light-hearted? As it turned out, He meant it in a very tangible way.

The directive seemed to be a call to live a slightly simpler lifestyle. It was time for me to lighten my load and not hold on to stuff. I wouldn't consider myself a Material Girl or a pack-rat by any means. However, I am quite sentimental. There were items I held on to for years because of their sentimental value alone. There were other things I had an unnecessary quantity of also. Okay, here's an example for full disclosure and understanding. I had too many purses and never used a fraction of them! Maybe you can relate. The quantity of shoes in your closet or the number of three-piece suits may be more than you reasonably need. Work with me, here. It makes me feel better to think I'm not the only one this principle could possibly apply to!

Once the intent of the word 'light' was clear, material things began to have much less significance. I remained conscious of the Lord's word to me all through the year. As each month passed I found myself being at peace donating items I thought I would keep a lifetime. The process of downsizing 'things' was not painful at all. I often told myself, "It must have a purpose or the Lord would not have asked me to do it".

As for being bold, it was a Holy boldness God was seeking from me. He had given me purpose and now was expecting me to act on it, regardless of whether I felt I was ready or not. I've mentioned several times throughout this book how I hesitated on giving someone a word from God. That could very well have been an area He wanted me to be a bit bolder in.

So often I tell people that grassroots efforts are just as impactful as global ones. We do not have to operate on a grand scale in order to fulfill our Kingdom purpose. Our sphere of influence, whether small or large, is what we are responsible for, that's it. I knew the Lord was telling me the season is 'now'. It was time to take additional steps towards fulfilling my

Kingdom purpose, and to be unashamed in doing it; be bold!

One year I missed His direction altogether. I recall telling a friend that I hadn't received my yearly direction from Him yet, even though I had sought Him for it. We were already a couple of months into the New Year. None of the previous years' messages had ever come this late. Little did I realize He had given it to me, but I missed it. I hadn't missed it because it was too complex to comprehend. I mentioned before God speaks to me in simple terms. Apparently, I missed it because the words were not spiritually prophetic sounding enough so what He said didn't register!

It took me until the third month of the year, after much reflection, to realize He had actually spoken it to me twice already. Since the words weren't packaged the way I thought they would be, I didn't see them for what they were. What He said was:

"Stop talking."

Can you see now how I may have been confused and missed it? "Stop talking". What in the world did God mean by that? Surely He wasn't asking me to take a vow of silence, was He? This was one I definitely had to seek understanding of!

I began to wonder if He saw me in a parallel view of the woman with the issue of blood. She did everything she could, spent all of her money seeking healing and wholeness from one source or another, all to no avail. As a matter of fact, scripture tells us that she grew worse! (Mark 5:26) What ended up helping was her faith and one touch of the Master's garment. She heard He was going to be near (accessible) and she sought Him out (Mark 5:27). The Lord is accessible to us but how much do we seek Him? He had the answer and she knew. We say we know God is all-knowing so why don't we go to Him more?

Was I talking too much and not seeking God enough about the issues of my life? It's easy to do. We need help figuring out financial matters so we seek out an advisor. It's hard raising a child as a single parent. Talking with other single parents can be comforting. Advice on how to move up in your company is best obtained from superiors in the organization, right? When having marital problems, it's good to talk with other couples who have overcome similar challenges, right? All of these life issues and more may be causing us to talk too much. Or at least, some of them may have been causing me to talk too much!

"Stop talking"; seriously?

I'll be transparent and admit this one was hard for me. My circle of trust is not a large one to begin with so I feel very comfortable talking to each person in it. I didn't think the Lord was suggesting I shouldn't trust them. My sincere belief is He just wanted me to come to Him more for guidance and advice. Scripture supports that in Psalms 118:8 "It is better to trust in the Lord than put confidence in man."

The instruction each year builds on the next. When the "light and bold" year was over, I did not lose sight of the instruction. I carried the mindset into the next calendar year as well. Likewise, I have been mindful to bring more of my conversation to the Lord after He asked me to "stop talking". The building blocks of each New Year advice have been used to create a mindset shift in me as to how to proceed with life.

There may come a year my New Year's guidance is meant to be specific to that year alone. So far, however, they have not been. Prayerfully I will know if it is. I am learning to listen and also striving to make it a practice to seek understanding in order to avoid misinterpretation.

Two months into the start of the next New Year, I was still kicking myself after occurrences when I realized the best thing I could have done was to simply "stop talking". I was able to reflect back and see how many times I could have saved myself issues had I simply not spoken certain things to certain people. It wasn't that what I said was wrong, rude, or harsh. It just didn't need to be said,

162

especially to particular people. At times it added to the confusion. At times what was said led to more confusion and misunderstandings; the very things I was attempting to clarify. At times they were not able to handle the information I wanted to share.

On a couple of occasions I can clearly remember trying to reach people by phone and wondering why I couldn't get any of them. In the car one day I was aggravated by a particular situation. I tried to reach my aunt. She was unusually inaccessible. I called my cousin and got her voicemail. There was no answer when I called my good friend either. After making those three attempts I took a mental pause. My next thought was, "Okay, Lord. You must want me to bring this matter to you instead of talking to anyone else about it."

Stop talking are words of wisdom essential to my personal and spiritual growth. It was a hard lesson to learn that year. I have a feeling I will be working on that one for a while!

There are numerous applications for this principle God gave me. With some Kingdom assignments, we have to move in silence until they are complete. It helps alleviate distractions, even the well-intentioned ones.

It is also becoming evident that our discussions about concerns and challenges may need to be limited. They can begin innocently enough: "I just need to vent." Have you ever said that? I have; many times. A friend will happily offer a listening ear. But how often has venting turned into an all-out complaining session? Some things simply are what they are. Do they deserve our time and energy? It can be counter-productive.

I am not suggesting we hold everything in or go to God only for everything. We should have trusted advisors and confidants in our lives. My advice would be to limit those "venting" conversations. Second, have them only with a person you know will help you keep the situation in perspective; someone who will encourage you appropriately.

Day 25 - Moment of Reflection:

Is there room in your life to talk less and seek God more?

_____

_____

_____

_____

_____

_____

_____

_____

_____

_____

_____

_____

_____

_____

_____

_____

_____

_____

_____

_____

Day 26

Survival by Faith

Survival by Faith is a book which never would have been written, let alone published, without the ability to listen/hear the voice of God.

If you've had a chance to read it, you are aware it chronicles a very painful period of my life. For a full calendar year, life consisted of one gut-punch after another. I became acutely aware the only way I was surviving the madness of life was by faith. If I relied on my feelings to get me through it all, I surely would not have made it.

166

During those twelve months, I sought God continually for understanding. And for twelve months, He never said a word. Lord knows I was listening; He just wasn't speaking. To my surprise, as soon as that particular hurtful year was over, He started talking. It was so clear to me what He was asking me to do, but I didn't want to, plain and simple. He was asking me to start writing down the experiences of the previous year. He didn't ask me once or twice. There was a constant calling for me to do this.

Having lived through the stressful situations, reliving them in vivid written detail was not a thought I relished at all. I've said before there is no testimony without transparency, so let me be transparent. I did not want to do it but was trying hard not to tell God no! My emotions were still raw and wounds had not yet healed. It seemed to me writing would be comparable to the pain of putting salt in a wound. Who, in their right mind, volunteers to do that?

Eventually, I relented to the persistent pull on my spirit. I gave in and began to write notes. The only rationale I could come up with was God must be planning to use this writing exercise as a healing mechanism for me. Over the years, writing had become a way for me to process feelings in order to move forward. In essence, I learned through the years that writing is therapeutic for me. Because I was so hurt from the events of the previous year, I finally agreed to start writing because I wanted to heal and move on with my life.

The year of trials, tests, and tragedies left me asking God many questions. "Why did I have to go through so much?" "What was I supposed to learn from it?" "Were these learning lessons, growth opportunities or consequences for wrongs I may have done?" These were some of the questions I asked for twelve months, only to be left to wonder the answers.

Once I made the decision to document my journey, God began providing answers to those questions. It turned out I was right in my presumption the assignment was for my healing. However, that was not the sole purpose of the assignment. The challenge to write was given so the Lord could show me what He was doing to me, for me, and through me in each of the situations encountered in the year I was asked to chronicle. In that process, healing did, in fact, begin to take place also. It became clear there was single-situation purpose, as well as a broader, collective purpose behind the events of that year. Most amazing of all is it was all for my good!

Learning to listen is important, and in this case, learning to wait to hear from God was critical. Seeking Him for direction and understanding for twelve months and hearing nothing back was difficult. My faith allowed me to hold on to hope that I would one day understand the reason(s) for it all. It didn't dawn on me that I would have to do anything other than ask in order to receive it.

I'm grateful I gave in to the persistent pulling on my spirit and started writing. Once the Lord deemed the timing right to answer my questions, it became evident He also intended my journey to be shared at large. This is how *Survival by Faith* came about.

When I think about the feedback readers have provided on how the book has blessed them with hope, encouragement, and strengthened their faith I am almost embarrassed I ever thought about telling God no. Saying no to God not only would have delayed my healing but it would have resulted in a continuation of frustration and despair for those who have received hope and faith from the book. How tragic that would have been!

God sees the big picture; we can scarcely see a snapshot of it. When He speaks, it is wise of us to realize He has our best interest in mind. Saying no certainly is an option. We were created with free will to do as we choose. No, however, probably is not the wisest response to give.

Had I said no,

1) I would not have received the answers I sought.

2) Those answers led to the healing I desperately needed.

3) Through the process, the book was born and has gone forth to bless many with hope.

At its basic level, you can look at this as a list of three bullet point by-products of listening to God. On a deeper, more meaningful level, these bullet points were life changing!

Tell God yes. You'll be glad you did! One simple yes has the potential to reveal, heal, and restore!

Day 26 - Moment of Reflection:

Have you had a 'no' moment with God, and do you view it differently now?

_____

_____

_____

_____

_____

_____

_____

_____

_____

_____

_____

_____

_____

_____

_____

_____

_____

_____

Day 27

Work

The majority of the short stories written so far have been personal in nature. God, however, does not limit Himself to guidance in our personal lives only. You read on Day 6 where I learned from what seemed to be God's denial about a work situation. He never actually spoke. When I did not get the job I sought, I perceived that as His 'no' to the job change. The story was a matter of discerning God's intent for me, waiting, and being patient to see how the entire situation would unfold. His 'no' was clear in that I did not get the job I desired. However, I simply didn't understand His 'no' meant there was something greater to come.

It's important for our spiritual growth and well-being to recognize, and be on alert for, the voice of God in every setting we are in. As I think of all the times hindsight revealed His guidance in my professional life, I am somewhat embarrassed at how often I have ignored it. I don't believe there has ever been a conscious thought that God isn't with me at work so I have not been able to figure out why I seem to be better at listening to Him elsewhere. I've wondered if it is because our relationship with Christ is so personal that it never dawned on me He would help me in my professional setting also. Regardless of the reason for not listening as much as I should have, I make a concerted effort to do so now.

Often times I will feel in my spirit that I should remind someone of a policy, procedure, or ask them to obtain more information about a matter before proceeding. Invariably, when I did not listen to the leading of the Holy Spirit, something came up later that could have been prevented had I followed through on what I felt in my spirit. Can I tell you how hard I kick myself in those moments! The first words that come to my mind in those instances are, "I knew it! Why didn't I say something?" Usually, the reason I hadn't is that I didn't want to give the person the impression I don't trust their decision making. At the same time, we have to become confident in God's leading. He would not put these things into our spirits if they were not for good purposes. As long as the feedback is given constructively and respectfully we should not drawback. We can be hindering someone's professional growth by not speaking up and sharing insight with them. Other ramifications are possible as well. Speaking up can avoid extra work later if something is caught and corrected early.

Our God is omnipresent. He is everywhere we are and everywhere we are not! His leading and guidance are just a prevalent at work as they are at home, in our personal lives, and in our relationships. He is limitless and the sooner we understand the fullness of that the better our lives will be. When something didn't go as well as it could have because I did not speak up but knew I was supposed to, all I can say is, "Lord, you tried to tell me.

Sorry!" I boxed Him out of my professional world with the mindset I created, whether consciously or subconsciously. The beautiful thing about God is He is persistent. Although I may not have listened as frequently as I should have, He never stopped speaking. I just had to learn to listen more. I'm grateful He blessed me with the opportunity to do so. That's grace!

Day 27 - Moment of Reflection:

Which area of your life are you currently boxing God out of?

_____

_____

_____

_____

_____

_____

_____

_____

_____

_____

_____

_____

_____

_____

_____

_____

_____

_____

Day 28

Missed Opportunity

It is pretty safe to say most authors are waiting for their big break. That moment one of their books receives national/international attention. All it takes is a single opportunity. Being in the right place at the right time, which means their steps were ordered there because there are no coincidences or chance encounters.

When an author is passionate about their book it is common for them to send copies to people with influence with they hope one of them will endorse it. When they strongly believe the book is one which will be a blessing to others, you can bet many authors have prayed and asked God to show them how to get it into the hands of those who can help propel it. I'm one of those authors!

My first book was sent to as many well-known men and women-led ministries across the country when it was first published. Although I did receive a couple nice 'best wishes for success' responses, it seems none of them were interested in assisting me to launch it more broadly. I can't be sure any of the books were ever seen by the bishops, pastors, evangelists, ministers they were addressed to. The letters I received back were from assistants and support staff.

A couple of years after it was published, I attended a national women's conference. It was hosted by a USA-based, internationally known minister. Her ministry is well respected. She, herself, has published numerous books. When I first became serious about living a life dedicated to Christ, her books helped me. Her writing style is straight-forward and her teaching principles are easy to apply to our everyday lives.

On the first day of the conference, as I parked my car in the garage, "something" told me to put one of my books in my purse. Without hesitation, I did so. I always keep some in the car with me. I obviously didn't know why the Holy Spirit was leading me to do that but I complied. Only good things come from His leading so I happily obliged.

Once I reached the arena there was time to spare before the program started. I was able to meet and talk with people who had come from all over the country for the conference. In one particular conversation with a woman from the Midwest, the subject of books actually came up. My initial, yet silent reaction was, "Ah ha! So this is why I was supposed to bring a book with me!" Although she was interested in hearing about the book she didn't ask about purchasing a copy and I didn't push it on her. So, I ended up carrying the book in my purse the whole day.

Before getting out of the car when I arrived for the second day of the conference activity, I took the book out of my purse and left it on the seat of my car. My purse had been heavy the day before and I wanted to lighten my

180

load. I removed the book and a couple of other items.

During the lunch break that day, I was sitting outside. While relaxing and basking in all of the great material presented in the first half of the day, I spotted a few people walking in my general direction. One of them looked familiar. With every step they took, the face of the woman in the middle became easier to see. She was the assistant to the minister hosting the conference! The only reason I recognized her was she had been on the stage each day giving a welcome to all of the attendees. She was walking leisurely, not in a rush, not shielded by security, and appeared very approachable. As the fullness of the opportunity began to register with me, I reached for my purse. A golden opportunity had presented itself. Here was my chance to put give a copy of my book to the influential woman by way of her right-hand woman!

As I picked up my purse, I suddenly remembered what I had done just a few hours earlier. I had taken it out and left it in the car! The golden opportunity was now a non-opportunity.

The Holy Spirit told me the day before to put a book in my purse. He did not tell me to take it out this day. That was all my doing! I listened without hesitation the day before but apparently decided whatever the Lord wanted to do was limited to the first day of the conference. The only thing I could do was sit there and literally shake my head!

With or without connecting to influential people, the Lord has the ability to make whatsoever He chooses a success. There are times He may elect to utilize relationships to further His work but it's not a requirement. I am simply acknowledging a potential missed opportunity as a result of my lack of sensitivity to the Holy Spirit in this story.

Day 28 - Moment of Reflection:

Do you have regret over a perceived missed opportunity? If so, please do not spend much time or energy focusing on it. What is meant to be will be!

_____

_____

_____

_____

_____

_____

_____

_____

_____

_____

_____

_____

_____

_____

_____

Day 29

When Rooming Goes Wrong

If you were raised with a strong sense of family, it can be easy to feel obligations towards them from time to time. Obligation, however, should never overrule what we know the Spirit of the Lord is telling us. If we allow it to, there is a great chance the situation will not work out well. Regret is inevitable.

A family member once asked if she could live with me for a few months. She was eager for a change and wanted to relocate to Florida. Part of me was excited; we had grown up very close and I loved her dearly. I was looking forward to having another family member living in the area. At the same time, there was a part of me that was quite unsure about agreeing to the arrangement. Our lifestyles were completely different which made me hesitant to say yes. As soon as she asked, my spirit became very uneasy. I was not accustomed to telling family "no" even though that's what I wanted to say. I also sensed in my spirit I was supposed to say no.

We were raised to help when able and that was pulling on me. I was in a position to help her. There wasn't a lot of extra room in my house but there was sufficient room to help for a transitional period of time. My house has been home to many over the years. Friends and family alike, when needed, have made temporary homes within mine. I've always considered it a privilege to help in that way.

The love I had for her in my heart had not diminished over the years so my uneasiness certainly was not indicative of that. I just knew in my spirit I was not supposed to say yes. For fear of disappointing her and giving the appearance I didn't want to help, I said yes and allowed her to move in.

Minus the disagreement my spirit had with the arrangement, the few months went well. We lived together just fine. Overall, she was a great houseguest. Yet and still, our lifestyles clashed and I was continually reminded by the Spirit of the Lord that the arrangement was not good for my household.

When the agreed-upon length of stay was drawing to a close she did not have a plan in place to move on. In conversation it became apparent she was hoping to extend her stay. I had already been disobedient to God's leading by saying yes in the beginning and was not willing to be disobedient again. I could not agree to an extension of her stay.

We had a discussion. We did not have an argument. Heated words were never exchanged. No ultimatums were given. I simply reiterated that the agreement had been for a specific period of time and that time was coming to an end. The discussion did not end with slamming of doors or anything of the sort. This is why I was surprised she moved out abruptly the following day.

She let me know that she moved in with a friend in a nearby town. It wasn't until other family members told me the truth. She went to a hotel and the story being provided to our family was quite different than the reality of the situation.

Our once close relationship was gone. To this day I am kept at arm's-length by her. She will speak if it is appropriate for the setting but will not initiate communication or contact. Because of how close we were, I thought this would change over time. It's been well over ten years and it has not. This is the result of my disobedience.

Had I said no to the living arrangement (as I knew I was supposed to) she probably would have been disappointed. I don't believe, however, that it would have ruined our relationship the way saying yes did.

When God speaks it is for our own good. We have to listen regardless of who is involved. Family is not exempt. He created our families so He is fully aware of what's best within the overall structure of it as well.

In this case, He spoke by placing such uneasiness in my spirit. I knew it. I recognized it. Obligation overruled it. The experience taught me a tremendously valuable and Biblically-based lesson:

Obedience is better than sacrifice.
(1 Samuel 15:22)

I don't want to sacrifice anymore relationships due to disobedience. Since then I have seldom done anything out of pure obligation, especially if I sensed in my spirit I shouldn't. I've also had to flat out say 'no' a couple of times when I knew the arrangement being proposed was ear-marked for confusion.

Day 29 - Moment of Reflection:

Can you recall a time when you felt you should decline participation in something but agreed anyway? How did it turn out for you?

_____

_____

_____

_____

_____

_____

_____

_____

_____

_____

_____

_____

_____

_____

_____

_____

_____

_____

Day 30

Our Thought Life Matters

The battlefield really is in our minds. Several good books have been published which teach the importance of our thought life.

One thought leads to another. Therefore it is vitally important to start with a good one! For example; on the way to work one morning I was thinking about my 'thought life' of late. I've been challenged to stay positive about a particular situation. A scripture came back to my remembrance while driving. I decided to focus on it for a while.

2 Corinthians 10:5 "…and bringing into captivity every thought to the obedience of Christ."

While meditating on the verse to see what revelation God was trying to give, several others scriptures starting coming to mind.

After arriving at work, God used my first thought as a springboard to a sequence of thoughts and it was amazing how they all tied together. I love it when He does that! I'm sure He loves when we allow Him to do that. 'Allow' in the sense of putting ourselves in position to let Him speak to us and us actually hearing what He said. Rest assured; God speaks frequently. However, we can be too busy and focused on other things that His voice is drowned out by the confusion around us.

I am grateful I was in position to hear Him this morning. Position does not necessarily refer to a physical place. At times it may. On this day, however, it was position of the spirit. I didn't want to have negative thoughts about the situation anymore; I sought God for help with it; I was actively waiting to hear from

Him. My spirit was in a position to receive
His guidance, and this is what He showed me:

- ❖ 2 Corinthians 10:5 "…and bringing
  into captivity every thought to the
  obedience of Christ." My first thought

- ❖ Proverbs 23:7 "As a man thinketh in
  his heart, so is he."

- ❖ Matthew 12:34 "Out of the abundance
  of the heart, the mouth speaks."

- ❖ Proverbs 18:21 "Death and life are in
  the power of the tongue."

Do you see the power of our thought life?

Our thoughts make deposits directly into our
hearts. Whatever we think on the most
becomes the abundance stored in our hearts.
The abundance is what we end up speaking
about, whether we realize it or not. The words
which we speak have the power to heal or kill.

Do you see how a first thought leads to so
many others? The first thought on this day
was positive and uplifting. One beneficial for

keeping me centered in Christ, regardless of what may come my way.

God helped guide my thoughts by placing these scriptures in my spirit because I left myself open for Him to do so. More often than not, as a result of us not seeking God, we try to guide our own thoughts. As the saying goes, "how'd that work out for you?"

What if my first thought had been one of defeat? What would the second thought and all others after that have been? It's likely they would have been more of the same.

When I made up in my mind to focus/study on 2 Corinthians 10:5 it was much easier for God to remind me of the subsequent ones. The first thought allowed a chain of positive thoughts to take place by way of scripture. The ones given to me were to help get my thought life back on track. What good would it have done for God to remind me of John 3:16? It would not have correlated to the issue at hand. God desired to show me, through scripture (which is the Believer's life instructions) how my thoughts matter and the extreme consequences they (my thoughts) can have if left unchecked!

When we are learning to listen to God, sometimes we have to pause and ask, "Okay, Lord. Is that it or is there more." That seemed to be the case on this day. After the first verse was given to me I wasn't clear how it related to the matter at hand. Giving myself quiet time to continue thinking, praying, and seeking about it, the Lord blessed me with (3) additional scriptures. They all tied together perfectly to help me realize my thought life had the potential to kill a situation I truly wanted to heal. The bottom line is to be patient. God may not give everything all at once, although sometimes He does. Learning is a continual process and God employs many methods to teach. There is no cookie-cutter approach to His teachings.

Day 30 - Moment of Reflection:

Think back to a time your thoughts were left unchecked. What was the end result?

_____

_____

_____

_____

_____

_____

_____

_____

_____

_____

_____

_____

_____

_____

_____

_____

_____

_____

Day 31

When He Leads, I Follow

The first book I was blessed to publish was completely Spirit-led. I often tell people I did not wake up one January morning and decide to start writing for the purpose of publishing a book. From the beginning, I was led by the Holy Spirit to document the journey I had taken in 2013. We fought one another for a short while because I did not want to write what I had experienced. Living it had been painful enough. The thought of re-living that year of my life through written words did not appeal to me. Thank God, however, I was eventually obedient to what I was being led to do (write)!

196

This book has been the opposite experience. While I do believe the Lord has given me full permission and the necessary anointing for this book, it was more my idea than His this time. He has shared so much with me through everyday life experiences, which I believe can be relevant eye openers for others as well. Since the book was mainly my idea I had a grand plan from the beginning as to when to publish it. My vision was to release the second book on the second anniversary of the first one, which would have been April 16th. If you've walked with the Lord any length of time you know that our timing is not always in line with His. But His timing is always best!

A few months before April I hit a wall; writer's block is the term often used. The book was so close to being finished, yet, despite my best efforts, I was at a complete standstill. Frankly, I was becoming frustrated. That's what happens when we focus on our plans versus seeking God for His. I didn't know why additional revelation was not coming to me and it never dawned on me to ask Him why. It would later become quite clear. There were experiences yet to come that need to be included in this book. Had I forced the issue and published it according to the timeline I set, it would not have the full content God desired. I had no way of knowing a major change in my life was approaching and He would have to lead me through it, step by step. Miraculous guidance was on the horizon, which was going to give me the strength and courage necessary to survive a turbulent time.

From the moment my career began in 1989, I knew I loved it. Event Management must be in my DNA. I have enjoyed a very long and largely fulfilling career in it for 30 years. Loving our profession does not exempt us from periodic challenges we must overcome. One of my most difficult ones came on Monday, April 30th. I was informed that my position was being eliminated.

Additionally, I was being placed back in the job I vacated six years prior. No warning. No discussion, just an instantaneous demotion! The position being eliminated was a Monday through Friday schedule. The position I was being placed in was one with no regular schedule. Years ago, I learned to say the only thing regular about my job was the irregular schedule. The job requires working evenings, weekends, holidays, and frequently, more than five days in a row before a day off.

There was no professional logic in the change that was being made. It seemed I was caught in the crossfire of the personal vendettas which included a game of "Who Has The Most Control". I felt as though I were a pawn in that game. It was ugly, painful, and the utmost of disrespectful. My life was flipped upside down during the course of a seven-minute conversation with my new manager.

What happened, why it happened, and the indignant manner in which it happened made me physically ill. In a matter of five days I lost enough weight for it to be visible and affect my daily clothes choices; not much fit! My emotions were out of control. I cried off and on for three weeks. None of what was taking place was by a fault of mine. Had I been demoted due to poor performance I could have accepted it better. The position I held for the past six years was a stepping stone towards higher positions. Therefore, being forced backward hurt tremendously. Maybe you've experienced something similar and can relate? When you love something and give your absolute all to it only to be used, the wound runs deep.

It seemed a certain group of people was being targeted. When I left work that day, I resolved within myself that I would be the one to stand up and fight the extreme injustices which had been taking place for quite a while. I went to bed that evening feeling broken but determined that, with the dawn of the next day, I would contest the wrong being done to myself as well as several before me.

When I woke the next morning (Tuesday), work was on my mind from the start. However, I tried to keep my normal routine which included reading my daily devotion. For a number of years, I have received one via email which makes it quick and convenient to read each morning.

To paraphrase, the devotion on this day was as follows:

> *Be quiet. Remain still. Keep emotions in check regardless of the situation. Fear not. Staying connected to the Lord will be crucial because*

He will keep you safe.

Scripture to study: Proverbs 29:25 "The fear of man brings a snare, but whoever trusts in the Lord shall be safe."

Lord have mercy! There was no coincidence happening here. I went to bed the night before intending to fight. This particular devotion was sent to provide my real marching orders; "Stand still and be quiet". Without any doubt, I knew the Lord sent this to me to let me know fighting was not what I was supposed to do. Let me be honest and tell you I was actually disappointed. Someone had to fight! None of the others before me did. The unfairness was sure to continue until someone said, "enough". I thought that someone was going to be me but God said otherwise.

As difficult as it was, I went to work that day and did my level best to do as told: "Stand still and be quiet." I managed to get through the day but not without tears, sadness, anger, and frustration. Why would God not let me fight? Others had lost their employment altogether.

I had been demoted and wasn't sure there was not a larger plan to eliminate me as well. It made me ill to see the damage that was being done in our workplace and to people's lives.

When the alarm clock went off Wednesday morning, I stuck with my routine and read the devotion even before getting out of the bed. In summary, it said:

> *Do not assume you know the end result of a situation. Remain in-tune with me spiritually despite any chaos taking place in the natural. My peace and strength are available to you.*

> *Scripture to study: John 14:27 "Peace I leave with you, My peace I give to you; not as the world gives do I give to you. Let not your heart be troubled, neither let it be afraid."*

I was utterly in shock at how specific the devotion was and how clearly it spoke to my present circumstances. "Refuse to project out to assume the future outcome…" I had been doing exactly that; assuming their plan was to ultimately terminate me or make me so uncomfortable and unhappy I would choose to leave. "The chaos that surrounds…" perfectly described the environment we were in at work.

As the week continued, so did the on-time messages. This is a re-cap of Thursday's devotion:

> *Let your spirit be renewed. I have much to give to you. Everything you need is at hand. Do not feel sorry for yourself or allow yourself to feel victimized. Stay focused on what is good and true. In the blink of an eye, I will bring you up from the pit as long as you stay focused on Me.*
>
> *Scripture to study: Colossians 3:2 Set your mind on things above, not on things on earth.*

It was becoming exciting, yet hard to comprehend, how each day's devotion was guiding me. The Lord was hand-holding me with His word and instructions! One of the predominant feelings I was struggling with was being a victim in the situation. Again, there was no valid reason for the change that had been taken place and it certainly was not pleasing to me. I felt completely and unfairly victimized. For Thursday's devotion to speak so clearly about not succumbing to the role of the victim was incredible to me.

In the months to come, I realized there was more involved than I realized in not playing the role of victim. Bitterness had set in and it caused me to operate outside of my God-given character at work. I had not become nasty or evil, matching the actions of others. I had, however, become distant. In addition, my naturally helpful disposition had turned such that I was forcing myself to not be helpful when I knew I could be and should be. None of that represents God well at all.

Letting go of bitterness took a weight off my shoulders I had no business carrying for such a long period of time anyway. The Lord had already told me everything would be alright. My duty then was to put my feelings aside and move forward in faith because I believed His promises to me.

Learning to listen encompasses so much more than just hearing from God. We have to first recognize His voice, hear what it is He is saying, and then apply it to all appropriate situations. The application tends to trip me up more than hearing. Maybe it's the same for you? The great news is God already knows where and when we will fall. I truly believe, however, that when our heart is right (wanting to do better), His grace will cover.

These devotions were saved intentionally so I could refer back to them from time to time when the environment at work seemed to contradict the promises God gave. They have proven to be rejuvenating. When God speaks to you, no matter the method, I encourage you to capture it in some way. Circumstances may not improve instantaneously or even as quickly as we think they should. Reflecting back on His promises to you provides strength to continue pressing forward until the promise comes. His promise to me was He would draw me up from the depths in an instant if I could seek Him and trust Him. It's hard to seek and trust with bitterness in my heart.

We closed out the week with this paraphrased devotion on Friday:

Wisdom and patience will help you review your options. By discernment you will know the climate of the spiritual atmosphere. The road ahead will be rough. Remain calm and of no fear; I've already made a way for you.

Scripture to study: Psalm 32:8 I will instruct you and teach you in the way you should go; I will guide you with My eye.

My God! The assurance this last devotion provided was exactly what I needed. The days ahead did not instantly get any better but the devotions, especially this one, helped me to know I would be okay. He had prepared the way for me! It would only be a matter of time! The email devotions the following week were not as prophetic as the ones shared here. What God gave me the next week instead were songs. Each morning I woke with a worship song in my spirit. The amazing thing is I did not go to bed the evenings before listening to any music. The content of the songs was more encouragement of who God is in our lives when we allow Him to be.

I had a plan to fight. God had a different approach and I was wise to heed to it. My inaction confused those who knew my desire to fight. There were a select few I knew could still be trusted and I had confided in them. The situation gave me an opportunity to explain my faith and trust in God. I count it a privilege to have had that opportunity. Seeds of faith were planted within them and I'm grateful for that. These people knew how adamant I was about fighting the injustice. To see me seemingly cower down was the perfect scenario to discuss obedience to Christ. The devotions may not have been shared with them but I certainly shared the impact of them!

The weeks and months ahead continued to be challenging. And, as of the time of this writing, the end result is still unknown. However, I have full confidence, based on what God spoke through those devotions, I will be alright!

Earlier I mentioned my goal was to release this book on April 16th. The upheaval did not occur until April 30th. This is why it could not have been published according to my timeline.

The way God used the daily devotions to speak and led me through that first week is what He wanted to include. The leading was too profound not to share with you! It's another beautiful example of the many ways He will speak if we will only listen.

Had I let the situation deter me from keeping my daily routine of reading the devotions, I would have been left to take matters into my own hands. As emotional as I was, I am certain that would have worked to my detriment. Regardless of how hard it may be, stay the course of life as much as possible when chaos abounds. Breaking my routine would have caused me to miss out on critical, divine guidance.

I was so lost that first week after the change at work. To realize the Lord loves us enough to provide step-by-step instructions to keep us safe left me more in awe of Him than I've ever been!

Day 31 - Moment of Reflection:

What has been the most profound way you've been led by God/received guidance from Him?

_____

_____

_____

_____

_____

_____

_____

_____

_____

_____

_____

_____

_____

_____

_____

_____

_____

_____

_____

Bonus Story: Who Am I

Early one Sunday morning I woke up and immediately had a question: 'Who Am I?' I didn't wake up with amnesia, so I wasn't asking because I didn't know my name, or know where I was at the moment. My profession wasn't a factor. My ethnicity was not a factor, nor my social status. It was bigger and deeper than that. It was more along the lines of 'Who is Shawn-Ta Wilson?' Who is the core person behind that name is what I seemed to be wondering that morning. I wanted to know on the deepest of levels.

What was more perplexing to me was why I woke with that as my first thought of the day. It was Mother's Day morning but I knew in my spirit I was not pondering the question in terms of who is Shawn-Ta Wilson as a mother. None the less, I apparently needed to process the question.

Because I put the question in the atmosphere, the Lord saw fit to answer it for me. As I've said many times, He's just good like that! His method of answering my question was so unique and beautiful that my mind didn't receive it for what it was at the moment. Before I knew it, I started thinking about a handful of truly amazing women who have made an impact on my life. I thought I was reminiscing about the ones who mothered me through the years simply because it was Mother's Day morning. In reality, God was speaking the answer to my early morning question. Initially, however, I was not able to recognize it as such. The more I thought about these wonderful women, the more I actually forgot the question I woke up with.

As I lay in the bed the Lord began reminding me of the character and qualities these women possessed. I held each fondly in my heart. Since it was Mother's Day, I decided to get up and write a tribute to them on Facebook. It was then, as I typed my thoughts and feelings about each one of them, that He showed me who I was. There are pieces of these women who make up the sum total of Shawn-Ta Wilson. I was blown away when He helped me to see a portion of them in me!

You just can't tell me that God is not real, or that He's not present with us on a daily basis, or that He won't provide what we need, even when all we need is an answer to a question.

As I looked at what I had written about them sincerely and from my heart, I felt a sense of fulfillment in knowing who I am. He took the best parts of them and poured it into me! After that, I was able to put my feet firmly on the floor that morning knowing precisely who I am!

Let me introduce you to them by sharing what was posted on Facebook that morning. After meeting them here, you will know who I am, all rolled into one woman, trying to be the best woman, mother, and daughter of the King I can be:

Valerie: My Mother. She loved her children and grandchildren deeply. She was a determined and dedicated woman but often misunderstood. If you were in need you could count on her to help, even without asking. She knew how to help me relax and distress just by feeding me and letting me rest when I went home to visit.

Alice. My Grandmother. The one who taught me so many lessons on what's right and wrong. She had expectations of me and I appreciated that. Time spent talking with her and doing her long, beautiful hair was priceless.

Margaret. My Grandmother. I saw her battle through one stroke after another, lose an adult son to drowning, another to murder, and her husband of many years to a car accident. To this day, I marvel at how she stayed strong and didn't crumble. I will forever remember her feisty and spirited nature because she gave it to me!

Hilda: My Aunt. She never had children of her own but I believe she adopted me in her heart. This became evident when my daughter Jordan came along. She took to her as if Jordan were her granddaughter; spending time with us, loving on us, and sending countless care packages to Jordan. And of course, there was Pittsburgh Steelers apparel in most of them. A football fan after my own heart!

Ms. Bernie: My friend and spiritual mentor. She had a huge, compassionate heart. Her energy seemed endless as she could never say no to a request for help. The love and laughter we shared over many meals will be with me forever.

By the time I finished typing the post that Mother's Day morning, I was in tears and could scarcely see the keyboard. I miss each of these women dearly, but I realized God left them with me – in me - forever. My heart was full of gratitude at that realization.

I could have easily sat home and cried all day that day, and I'm sure everyone would have understood. My mom had only been gone for three months. I'm so glad I did not dismiss the question in my spirit that morning. If I had, I would never have known what God wanted me to see about myself. He was trying to tell me something and He needed me to listen. He could have woken me up any day with that question in my spirit, but He chose Mother's Day because He knew I would be primed to listen.

The experience of that morning left me feeling all the more grateful for His love, and for the wonderful women He put in my life, who helped shape me into who I have grown to be, and still strive to be more like.

I asked; He answered, and I listened.

I'm glad I was able to connect these two incidents and not see them as isolated occurrences. I asked a question and God graciously answered it. I am thankful I was listening and understood what He showed me about those women was connected to the question of "Who Am I".

Who Am I? I wanted to know on the deepest of levels. My profession didn't matter when thinking of that question. My residential status as a Floridian didn't matter. Who people know me as didn't matter either. My desire was to know what I am made of that makes me who I am. And He showed me exactly that!

Bonus Story - Moment of Reflection:

Do you believe God will answer your
questions?

_____

_____

_____

_____

_____

_____

_____

_____

_____

_____

_____

_____

_____

_____

_____

_____

_____

_____

_____

_____

Final Thought

My writing has been referred to as simplistic and I love that! Life is complex enough. My prayer is that these short stories will assist you in being able to recognize the leading of the Holy Spirit in your life as well. He is our Helper; to lead, guide, teach, and reveal to us.

The basis from which Speak Lord has been written is to show how we can discern His voice from our own, and even from that of the enemy.

The instincts or intuitions we have are given to us by the Holy Spirit because of God's love

218

for us. His desire is to see us be well in all areas of our lives. Don't ignore His gentle whisper and soft nudging. It is always for our good as well as the good of others.

He will never lead us to speak a word which will cause undue harm to someone or create strife. Truth, spoken in love, may still generate strife if the person is not ready to receive the truth. This is a different matter, however.

The many personal stories written are with the purpose of showing how involved God is in our day-to-day lives. Look for and embrace His guidance.

About the Author

Simply stated, Shawn-Ta Sterns Wilson is a woman who has decided to follow Christ and His will for her life. She believes part of her calling is to provide encouragement to strengthen individuals in their daily lives and their faith. Writing has provided an avenue for her to do exactly that.

Shawn-Ta gives all credit to God for her writing. He continually shares revelation with her which allows her writing to be impactful and inspiring. Shawn-Ta's stories, based on life experience, are relatable, spiritually uplifting, and encouraging to readers. Her transparent style of writing allows readers to connect with her immediately. Shawn-Ta believes "there is no testimony without transparency".

When asked about writing Shawn-Ta says, "I use it as a means to show people how accessible and present God is in our day-to-day lives". Her first book, *Survival by Faith*, has touched many lives. In addition to being an author of books, she is a staff writer with The Lyfe Magazine.

Born in Connecticut and raised in Virginia, Shawn-Ta now resides in Florida. She is a Certified Meeting Professional (CMP) and her career in the convention industry spans thirty years. In that time she has successfully managed events ranging in size from ten to 20,000 people. Her professional experience includes a special assignment with the 1996 Olympic Games in Atlanta, Georgia. Her expertise in her chosen career field was acknowledged when she received the nationally awarded Convention Services Manager of the Year award. In her words, however, "the greatest award I've ever received was the title of Mom to my daughter".

Shawn-Ta finds enjoyment in the simple pleasures of life. Those things we often times may take for granted: quality time with family and friends; watching a stunning sunrise or captivating sunset; the peace and quiet of a secluded beach.

For a daily dose of encouragement, follow Shawn-Ta on social media:

Facebook:
www.facebook.com/survivalbyfaith

Instagram:
www.instagram.com/shawnta_the_writer

 Thank You!

I would like to take this opportunity to thank you for reading my book, *Speak Lord, I'm Learning to Listen.*

Please consider reading my previous book, *Survival by Faith,* as well. I also write for "The Lyfe Magazine", a Christian lifestyle publication, if you would like to read my monthly articles.

Last, if you enjoyed this book, please go to your favorite bookseller's site and write a review of it for me. Reviews increase visibility of novels on these sites making them easier for other readers to find.

Thank you so much and always be blessed!

Shawn-Ta

Made in USA - Kendallville, IN
1068853_9780578524436
04.02.2020 1850